# CRYPTOCURRENCY FOR COMPLETE BEGINNERS

THE ULTIMATE INVESTOR'S GUIDE TO BITCOIN, ETHEREUM, ALTCOINS, NFTS, AND BLOCKCHAIN. LEARN TO INVEST SMART, MANAGE RISK, AND RIDE THE NEXT MILLIONAIRE-MAKING WAVE

LUCAS STERLING

TOP TIER PRESS

Published under the author brand **Lucas Sterling**

# CONTENTS

RYPT

R COMPL

GINN

# INTRODUCTION

Imagine you're standing at the edge of a vast, mysterious landscape. In the distance, you hear about fortunes being made, new tools for creative freedom, and even money that moves at the speed of thought. The word "crypto" echoes everywhere from your friends' WhatsApp chats to headlines on your social media feeds to late-night conversations with colleagues who say, "I just bought some Bitcoin." On one hand, it sounds thrilling, a whole new world of possibility. On the other hand, all the noise and jargon make it feel risky, complicated, and maybe even a little bit scary.

You might be wondering: Is cryptocurrency really worth my attention? Isn't this just another overhyped trend people will laugh about in five years? Am I too late, or worse, already left behind?

Let's be clear from the outset: cryptocurrency is more than just hype. It's a revolution quietly reshaping how people around the world think about and use money. For decades, we've relied on banks and middlemen to move value across borders, to store our savings, or to power new businesses. However, cryptocurrency has managed to unlock those previously unattainable opportunities. Suddenly, anyone with a smartphone and an internet connection, no matter where they live, can participate in this new financial universe.

Why is this such a big deal? For the first time in modern history, ordinary people, not governments or mega-corporations, are rewriting the rules of money. You don't need a PhD, a Wall Street job, or even prior experience investing. Crypto puts powerful financial tools in your hands, inviting you to join a global experiment in innovation, ownership, and opportunity.

But let's be honest: if you're reading this, there's a good chance you're feeling overwhelmed. Every search for "crypto investing" seems to reveal a plethora of technical terms, including blockchains, wallets, miners, forks, NFTs, DeFi, and more. One blog says you're missing out if you don't buy today. Another warns it's all a giant bubble. And every guide feels written for either rocket scientists or reckless gamblers, not careful, curious beginners like you.

That's why this book exists: to cut through the chaos, demystify the basics, and give you a solid foundation, regardless of your background. You don't need to know anything about programming, finance, economics, or cryptography. If you can use a smartphone and shop online, you have everything it takes to understand and benefit from the crypto movement.

So, what will you gain from these pages? Three things: understanding, action, and confidence.

First, you'll learn the "why" behind cryptocurrency, not just what it does, but why it matters. We'll start with simple stories and real-world examples: sending money overseas without sky-high fees, protecting your savings from inflation, or artists selling digital masterpieces directly to fans without big tech platforms taking a cut. You'll see how blockchain technology works without getting lost in complicated algorithms or code.

Second, we'll focus on practical steps. This isn't theory; it's your beginner's handbook. You'll discover how to safely set up your first digital wallet, choose and buy your first coins, keep your investments secure, and dodge the most common scams and mistakes. No step will be skipped. Each explanation is broken down into plain English, as if I were walking you through it, side by side.

And finally, you'll walk away with confidence. Crypto can be volatile and confusing, but it doesn't have to be intimidating. Knowledge is your shield against hype, fear, and impulsive decisions. By the end of this book, you'll know which risks to watch out for, how to spot red flags, and how to grow your position slowly and smartly. You'll be able to join the conversation about digital assets not just with curiosity, but with clarity and poise.

Now, if you've ever felt like learning about crypto is like cracking some secret code, let me reassure you: jargon stops here. You won't find any unnecessary acronyms, heart-pounding price charts, or endless rabbit holes of tech-speak. Everything you need to get started is explained in down-to-earth language, using everyday analogies and plenty of real-life scenarios. When terms come up, and sometimes they must,

I'll break them down on the spot, so nothing slips by unnoticed or unexplained.

Who is this book for? For anyone who's ever watched from the sidelines, wishing they could ask "dumb questions" without judgment. For the careful, cautious investor who wants to build wealth and security, not chase quick thrills. For young professionals looking to diversify their portfolios beyond traditional stocks and bonds. For freelancers, artists, and entrepreneurs curious about new ways to create and get paid. For anyone tired of feeling locked out of important financial conversations simply because they don't speak the lingo.

If you've already tried searching for answers online, you know how easy it is to drown in conflicting advice. One influencer screams, "BUY NOW!" while another swears everything is doomed. Reddit threads spiral into memes and inside jokes. You're left more confused than when you started. Here, you'll find an island of calm: straightforward guidance, real facts, and actionable steps, nothing more, nothing less.

Let me also make a promise: it's okay to be skeptical. You should ask tough questions. Not everything about crypto is golden, and yes, there are risks. There have been scams, wild price swings, and exaggerated promises. This book will show you both the bright opportunities and the pitfalls, the exciting innovations and the traps to avoid. With the right knowledge, you'll steer clear of costly mistakes and hype-driven panic.

So, whether you want to buy your first Bitcoin, learn what Ethereum actually does, explore NFTs and digital art, or simply understand what all your friends are talking about, you're in the right place. Together, we'll tackle everything step by step, building your confidence and turning the unknown into something familiar and even empowering.

You don't have to leap headfirst into the wild world of crypto. You just have to take the first step, armed with the right information and a sense of curiosity. My goal is to turn your caution into clarity and your intrigue into action. Let's pull back the curtain, cast aside the jargon, and see what the future of money really looks like.

Ready? Your journey into the world of cryptocurrency starts here, and it's for everyone, especially you.

# UNLOCK YOUR CRYPTO MASTERY TOOLKIT

*Ready to take control of your digital wealth with clarity and confidence?*

As a thank-you for reading this book, I've created a practical guide: **The Crypto Mastery Toolkit.** This hands-on guide simplifies key crypto concepts, helps you secure your assets, and builds confidence as you manage your digital wealth. It's designed to help you learn and apply crypto knowledge with ease and clarity.

*What's included in this resource:*

- Understand key crypto concepts and terminology
- Learn strategies for secure asset management
- Discover best practices for wallets, exchanges, and safety
- Develop confidence navigating today's digital economy

**Access Your Companion Workbook**

Visit: **https://content.toptierpress.com/unlock-free-crypto-mastery-toolkit**

Or scan the QR code below to get instant access!

# CHAPTER 1
# WHAT IS CRYPTOCURRENCY, REALLY?

Well over 2 billion people worldwide still lack access to traditional banking services, yet many of them carry smartphones capable of connecting to the internet. Imagine sending money across borders without waiting days or paying high fees, or owning a form of currency that isn't controlled by any government or bank. This is no longer just a possibility; it's happening every day through cryptocurrency. But what exactly is this digital money, and how does it work when there's nothing physical to hold or a bank teller to visit? The basic differences between cryptocurrency and the cash we use daily can feel confusing at first, especially if you're new to finance or technology. Yet beneath the surface lies a system built on transparency, security, and freedom that challenges the way we think about money. This chapter takes you inside the basics of cryptocurrency and blockchain technology, offering clear insights into why these innovations matter today and why millions are beginning to see crypto as more than just headlines or hype.

## Understanding Cryptocurrency: How It Differs from Regular Money and How Blockchain Works

Money has always meant something you can hold in your hand or see in your bank account. Dollars, euros, and yen are familiar because they come as coins, bills, or numbers controlled by banks or governments. Cryptocurrency flips this idea. There is no stack of crypto coins in anyone's pocket. Everything happens online, using computer codes. Bitcoin, Ethereum, and other cryptocurrencies exist because people agree to recognize streams of numbers and letters as valuable, not because some treasury created them or a bank approves each transaction.

The control of traditional money sits with governments and central banks. When the government prints dollars or the European Central Bank manages euros, they can influence how much is in use. Cryptocurrency, on the other hand, isn't managed by any country or company. The rules are built right into the software itself. Anyone with access to the internet can use crypto. There is no branch manager, bank teller, or official anywhere who decides who gets to join or what they can do. Instead, computer networks run by regular people all over the globe take care of everything through code.

The supply is another big difference. Central banks can choose to create new money whenever they believe it's needed, which sometimes leads to inflation. With Bitcoin, the maximum amount that will ever exist is set from the very beginning. There will never be more than 21 million Bitcoins. The software controls this, and nobody can change it. Some other cryptocurrencies set their limits in different ways, but the core idea is that the rules about new money creation are transparent and can't be quietly altered.

Crypto is also borderless. Picture trying to send money from one country to another. With regular money, you might need to deal with transfer fees, exchange rates, and waiting days for everything to clear. Cryptocurrency can be sent anywhere, to anyone, day or night, with just a digital address and an internet connection. There are no weekends or bank holidays in this world.

All cryptocurrencies depend on blockchain technology. To grasp how a blockchain works, think of a ledger, like the kind old shopkeepers used, but imagine it's not stored in one dusty back room. Instead, thousands of people have the exact same copy on their computers. Every time someone sends or receives cryptocurrency, the transaction is written in the ledger. New transactions are gathered together in groups called "blocks." A block might contain dozens or hundreds of transactions.

Once a block is full, it's locked and added to the chain of blocks; that's where the name "blockchain" comes from. Every computer with a copy of the ledger checks over this new block to make sure everything adds up and that nobody is trying to fake a record. This checking process is public and open. If someone tries to lie, like claiming to have more Bitcoin than they do, the other computers will ignore it because it doesn't match their records. This setup makes cheating almost impossible.

Imagine this: Bob wants to send Alice some Bitcoin. He opens his crypto app, types in Alice's digital address, and enters the amount. His app puts the details together and sends them out to the network. Each computer on the network checks, "Does Bob really have enough Bitcoin?" If the answer is yes, Bob's balance goes down, and Alice's position goes up in the shared ledger. A record of the payment joins a group of other transactions inside a block. Soon, that block is added forever to the blockchain, where anyone in the world can see it.

People use cryptocurrencies for more than sending money. Some buy their morning coffee using crypto by scanning a code at checkout if the café accepts it. Others use cryptocurrency apps to send money home to family in another country. These transfers arrive in minutes, and the fees are often far lower than with regular banks or Western Union. Many see crypto as a way to invest, hoping the price of Bitcoin or Ethereum will rise so they can sell later at a profit. Digital art, collectibles, and even tickets to events are now bought and sold using crypto.

Trust in cryptocurrency comes from how open the system is. The rules are set in public software that anyone can search and inspect. All transactions are visible on the blockchain for everyone to check, so there are no hidden changes or back room deals. The security of the network comes from thousands of computers cross-checking every transaction, making it far harder for anyone to cheat or control the system alone.

Learning what sets cryptocurrency apart from regular cash opens the door to bigger questions. Crypto isn't just a new way to pay for things or a digital coin to invest in. Its open, shared, world-spanning design offers a new vision for how people move value and make agreements. More ideas about openness, choice, and even the freedom to run your own financial life start to come into view, inviting you to see what else might be possible.

## The Importance and Impact of Crypto: Decentralization, Transparency, Freedom, and Real-World Applications

Cryptocurrency stands out because it offers something people have rarely had before: true control over their money in a digital world. With traditional banks, a few powerful players decide the rules. They can block or delay transactions, add fees, limit access during crises, or freeze accounts. Cryptocurrency reverses this through decentralization, a big word for a simple idea. No single person, company, or government acts as the boss. Instead, many computers worldwide run the network, each sharing the job and checking on the others.

Imagine sending money to a family member overseas. With banks, the money passes through several stops, each adding costs and delays. Cryptocurrency, such as Bitcoin or Ethereum, allows people to send funds directly, often in minutes, with much smaller fees. There is no gatekeeper slowing things down.

Decentralization also means equal access. Older systems sometimes shut people out, such as those without the right paperwork to open a bank account or anyone trapped by unstable policies in their home country. Picture a woman running a small business where banks are unreliable or corruption is common. By using cryptocurrency, she can protect her earnings, pay suppliers in other countries, and join a global market. Her story looks different because she no longer relies on a single company or government to control her financial future.

This network structure also makes cryptocurrency fairer. No single actor can decide who gets to use the system or change the rules behind closed doors. For people in countries facing runaway inflation or strict financial controls, this can mean holding money that keeps its value instead of watching savings disappear overnight. It offers a real chance to bypass middlemen, placing more hope and resources in the hands of ordinary people.

Transparency works differently in cryptocurrency than in banks or most companies. Each transaction lives on the blockchain, a public digital record that anyone can inspect. Although wallets use anonymous addresses instead of names, the movement of money is visible to everyone. This makes fraud or double spending much harder to carry out unnoticed. For example, a charity can share its donation address, allowing anyone to see when funds arrive and how they are spent. Donors can follow their money's journey step by step, which builds trust.

Ethical supply chains also benefit from this transparency. Imagine buying a bag of coffee. Retailers could include a code that lets customers trace the beans' entire path from farm to factory to store shelf directly on the blockchain. This helps shoppers avoid products linked to unfair labor or environmental harm and shifts power toward honest producers and informed consumers.

Financial freedom is much more than a catchphrase when traditional financial systems exclude or restrict millions. Consider a refugee resettling in a new country, unable to open a bank account due to missing paperwork. With a simple smartphone, they can create a digital wallet, store savings in cryptocurrency, and join economic life faster than any paperwork would allow. For many, cryptocurrency becomes a tool for basic dignity, not just investment.

Beyond these core ideas, the practical uses of cryptocurrency and blockchain reach into many parts of everyday life. Sending remittances, or money sent home by workers abroad, often involves high fees, long waits, and heavy paperwork. Crypto tools make this process faster and cheaper, allowing instant low-cost transfers almost anywhere in the world. Services like Litecoin or Stellar can move money in seconds, often for just a few cents per transaction. For families living far apart, this kind of access can be a lifeline.

Many people around the world still lack traditional banking services. They may have smartphones but no checking or savings account. Cryptocurrency offers them a way to save, pay, and borrow using only a digital wallet and an internet connection. Microloans, insurance, and other financial services can run through smart contracts, which are automatic programs on the blockchain that replace middlemen with transparent and consistent rules.

Digital creators find new ways to control and profit from their work too. Artists and musicians sell their art directly using NFTs (non-fungible tokens), proving ownership and getting paid without big corporations as middlemen. Someone who draws or makes music can sell directly to fans, who in turn can verify they own the real thing.

Decentralized finance, or DeFi, lets anyone lend, borrow, or earn interest with just a digital wallet. There's no need to ask a bank manager or face tough loan rules. You use platforms where the code handles everything, and everyone can see the rules.

The real shift lies in who gets to join and benefit from digital and financial systems. Blockchain ensures that no single player holds all the power. Openness, where anyone can see, verify, or build something new, leads to fairer systems. From tracking goods in shipping to securing elections against tampering and making global trade smoother, blockchain technology is already proving its impact across many industries. While price fluctuations often dominate the headlines, the deeper story of blockchain is about freedom, trust, and access. These ideas have the potential to transform far more than just money.

Now that we understand how cryptocurrency differs from traditional money and the role blockchain technology plays, we can see why this digital shift matters. Crypto offers a new way to control and move money without relying on banks or governments, opening doors for anyone with internet access to participate in a global financial system. Its transparency, security, and borderless nature provide tools for greater freedom, fairness, and opportunity, especially for those often left out of traditional finance. As you start your journey into buying and investing in crypto, this foundation gives you the confidence to navigate the space wisely, avoid common pitfalls, and explore the many ways digital assets might fit into your financial future.

CHAPTER 2

# MEET THE STARS – BITCOIN AND ETHEREUM

"Why should I trust something that isn't printed by a bank or backed by a government?" That's a question many people ask when they first hear about Bitcoin and Ethereum. It's natural to feel cautious about digital money that exists only on the internet, especially if you're new to cryptocurrency. But behind this new form of value lies more than just virtual coins. It represents a revolution in how we think about money, ownership, and trust.

These two cryptocurrencies have captured the world's attention because they offer radically different ways to manage finance and technology without relying on traditional institutions. Understanding their unique roles is essential to making smart choices in the fast-changing world of crypto. This chapter will guide you step by step through what makes Bitcoin and Ethereum stand out, helping you understand why millions of people around the globe are beginning to rely on them.

## Understanding Bitcoin and Ethereum: Their Strengths, Roles, and Market Dominance

Bitcoin began as the world's first cryptocurrency, launched in 2009. At its core, Bitcoin offers a digital form of money that isn't managed by any one government, company, or person. This structure means no central bank can print more of it or devalue what people already own. Bitcoin's code sets a maximum of 21 million coins that will ever exist. People sometimes call it "digital gold" because, just like gold, Bitcoin offers scarcity and a reliable way to hold value over time even when traditional banks struggle or currencies lose strength.

For many people in countries facing political or financial turmoil, banks may freeze assets, limit withdrawals, or prevent money transfers abroad. Bitcoin helps anyone bypass these limits. Owning Bitcoin means controlling your money directly, since only you hold the "keys" to your funds. Even if a government tried to censor transactions, the Bitcoin network's design makes it nearly impossible to block or reverse a legitimate transfer. People have sent Bitcoin across borders during times of crisis when wallets, banks, or even physical cash were unavailable. Wherever the internet reaches, Bitcoin transactions can go there too.

Security is another feature that draws people to Bitcoin. The system keeps track of all coins and transfers through a shared digital ledger called a blockchain. Thousands of computers all over the planet work together to verify every transaction, and once a transfer is recorded, it can't be changed or faked. This setup makes stealing Bitcoin or forging its history extremely difficult. At the same time, no individual or organization can interfere with the network's basic rules. All these aspects create a sense of reliability for those looking to protect their wealth against inflation or unstable economies.

While Bitcoin focuses mainly on being a secure and limited store of value, Ethereum takes the idea of digital money and expands what's possible. Imagine a vending machine: you put in money, make a selection, and the machine immediately gives out your snack if you've paid the right amount. No shopkeeper needs to stand by the machine that runs the transaction as a fixed rule. Ethereum uses a digital version of this logic called a smart contract. A smart contract is a bit of blockchain-based code that runs exactly as programmed, handling agreements and transactions automatically without the need for a third party.

Ethereum's platform lets anyone create these self-executing contracts, which power a growing ecosystem of decentralized tools and applications. These range from online games and social clubs to peer-to-peer lending and digital art markets. One of the largest changes Ethereum brought was making it easier for people to build new ideas on top of a blockchain. This has unlocked industries like NFTs, which certify ownership of digital items (such as artwork), and DeFi (Decentralized Finance), which offers banking tools without involving a bank at all. Whether it's borrowing, lending, trading, or launching a new kind of software, developers build these services thanks to Ethereum's programmable foundation.

Bitcoin and Ethereum hold the top two spots in the world of digital assets. Each plays a special role:

Bitcoin stands out because:

- It's the most widely recognized cryptocurrency in the world
- People trust its safety record and steady supply
- It's often used as a "set and forget" store of value, much like putting savings in a solid safe

Ethereum stands out because:

- Its technology enables new types of applications, not just currency
- Innovators can launch products and services directly on Ethereum's network
- Its system is more flexible, letting new features and projects grow rapidly

Bitcoin often leads the market because of its history, stability, and simple goal: be digital gold. Investors see it as a reliable starting point, and it tends to drive public confidence in cryptocurrency. Ethereum, by contrast, is seen as the playground for builders and creators. That's why most of today's action, products, and trends in crypto come from the world of Ethereum.

Both coins lead the market by total value held and traded by people worldwide. This dominance makes them the first choice for new users, while most businesses offering crypto payments support these two before others. The large communities and vast amount of information around Bitcoin and Ethereum help protect beginners from the risks that come with lesser-known currencies.

Getting to know the basic features and strengths of Bitcoin and Ethereum is a wise entry point for anyone exploring cryptocurrency. Their success has encouraged a wave of trust and mainstream interest, giving newcomers a safer path, solid information, and less risk of falling into scams. By focusing on their main purposes, digital gold for saving, and a smart, flexible platform for building beginners can make decisions with more clarity.

Bitcoin and Ethereum might lead together, but what sets them apart in everyday use and which fits different needs best? The next step is examining their practical differences and how each shines in real-world situations.

## Key Differences Between Bitcoin and Ethereum with Real-World Use Cases

Bitcoin and Ethereum may seem alike at first because both use blockchains and allow people to send value digitally, but their technologies work in distinct ways that shape how they are used in everyday life. Bitcoin's system centers around one core goal: to record transactions in a way that is secure, trustworthy, and almost impossible to change. Every block in Bitcoin's blockchain is a simple record of transactions such as "Alice sent 1 BTC to Bob" or "Carol received 0.5 BTC from Dave." The entire network is built around a single question: can everyone trust that these records are accurate and permanent? By focusing only on transactions, Bitcoin keeps things simple and solid, earning its reputation as "battle-tested."

Ethereum was built from the start to do much more. Its blockchain doesn't just track who sent what to whom. It also contains small programs called smart contracts. These contracts are pieces of code that sit inside Ethereum's blocks and carry out instructions automatically. Unlike Bitcoin, Ethereum's system is like a digital computer that anyone can use to build applications. When someone writes a smart contract, they essentially upload a robot employee who works on the blockchain, following orders without mistakes or taking sides. This makes Ethereum flexible. People can invent new kinds of agreements, build online games, make digital art, or even create entire banking systems, none of which could work on Bitcoin.

## Comparing Use Cases

The result is a split in what each platform is best known for. Bitcoin is considered a store of value, the digital version of gold. Its main purpose is to keep value safe and let it move across borders without asking anyone's permission. People use it to save money, send it to family across the world, or protect their savings in places where banks aren't safe. Companies and even a few countries keep part of their financial reserves in Bitcoin because its supply is limited. You can imagine someone in Argentina wanting to save in something safer than the local currency; putting their savings into Bitcoin can help shield them if their money loses value quickly. Or think about a family member in the United States sending Bitcoin home to relatives; they might skip the slow, expensive bank process, and the fees disappear.

Ethereum, on the other hand, is more like a playground for new ideas in finance, art, and business. It's used to build programs that can create, trade, or manage digital goods. Ethereum powers platforms where you can lend money, earn interest, swap tokens, or trade digital collectibles called NFTs (non-fungible tokens). For instance, an artist draws a digital painting, creates an NFT of it on Ethereum, and sells that NFT through a global marketplace. The buyer then owns the official, unique version of the digital art. Or a programmer might code a lending app where users can borrow and lend money out, fully automated by smart contracts, never needing a bank in the middle.

## Real-World Scenarios

To see the difference in action, imagine two friends: Maya and Lucas. Maya lives in Canada but wants to send money to her parents in the Philippines every month. She buys Bitcoin, sends it straight to her family, and they exchange it for local money. The transaction takes moments, costs very little, and avoids bank delays.

Lucas is a graphic designer who creates digital posters and wants to sell them globally. He uses Ethereum to mint NFTs for his artwork. Through an NFT marketplace, collectors buy these pieces, and the smart contract ensures Lucas gets paid right away. Lucas never had to open a shop or worry about international payment systems; Ethereum handled it all.

## Key Industries Using Bitcoin and Ethereum

A few industries rely on Bitcoin and Ethereum in strikingly different ways:

**Finance**

- **With Bitcoin:** People and businesses use it for fast, secure international payments or as a hedge against unstable national currencies.
- **With Ethereum:** The world of decentralized finance (DeFi) lives here. Borrowing, lending, trading, all happen automatically through smart contracts, with no middleman.

**Art & Collectibles**

- **With Ethereum:** NFTs let artists prove ownership and sell digital creations. Buyers can securely trade these assets, knowing the smart contract locks in the rules of the exchange.

**Supply Chains**

- **With Ethereum:** Companies write smart contracts so every step of a shipment is tracked, recorded, and visible. This brings honesty and proof into how goods move from maker to buyer, cutting the risk of fraud.

While both Bitcoin and Ethereum use blockchains to change how people move value and information, the backbone of each platform means they fit different roles. Bitcoin is steady and reliable, a place to save money or send it safely. Ethereum is for building, experimenting, and running new kinds of applications. Knowing how these differences work in everyday life helps investors and users make better choices in the world of crypto.

Now that we have explored the unique strengths and real-world uses of Bitcoin and Ethereum, newcomers can better understand how these two leading cryptocurrencies fit into today's digital economy. Bitcoin offers a secure, trusted way to save and transfer value across borders, much like digital gold, while Ethereum opens doors for creative applications, from finance to art, through its smart contract technology. With this foundation, readers are ready to make informed choices about which platform suits their personal goals and risk tolerance. By focusing on what each coin does best, anyone curious about crypto can move forward with greater confidence, avoiding common pitfalls and stepping into the world of digital assets with clarity and purpose.

CHAPTER 3

# ALTCOINS EXPLAINED (AND WHICH TO WATCH)

More than 10,000 cryptocurrencies are available today, yet only a handful have lasting value and real-world use. For many newcomers, the world of altcoins and any digital currency beyond Bitcoin can feel overwhelming and confusing. Different coins promise faster payments, stronger privacy, or new ways to use money online. But behind every name and ticker symbol lies a story about who created it, what purpose it serves, and whether it's built to last or just chasing attention. Many people dive in hoping to catch a quick win but end up lost amid hype, hidden risks, and unclear goals. Understanding how to tell which altcoins are meaningful and which ones carry danger is key to making smart, confident choices as you explore the growing crypto landscape. This chapter will guide you through that process step by step.

## Understanding Altcoins and Their Types

The word "altcoin" simply means any cryptocurrency that is not Bitcoin. Bitcoin came first, and its purpose was clear: a trusted electronic form of money not controlled by governments or banks. Shortly after Bitcoin's launch, developers and entrepreneurs began designing alternatives for all sorts of new uses and ideas. That's where "alt," meaning "alternative," comes from. Altcoins aren't just copycats; they are digital currencies and tokens built to solve problems, fill gaps, or experiment with new technology. Some are very different from Bitcoin, while others just tweak how it works. For anyone new to crypto, it's useful to see Bitcoin as the original and altcoins as all the new digital currencies that came after.

Altcoins exist because Bitcoin, while groundbreaking, does not do everything. After Bitcoin's rise, creators saw opportunities for coins with faster transaction speeds, greater privacy, new security options, or even ways to program rules right into their currencies. As a result, the crypto world started to grow rapidly, with each altcoin carving out its own possible use. Ethereum is a leading example. Instead of focusing only on payments, Ethereum introduced "smart contracts," self-running software programs that complete deals or handle transactions according to rules you set. These smart contracts opened the gate for new online businesses and applications. Litecoin arrived as a "lighter" Bitcoin, aiming to process transactions more quickly and cheaply. Dogecoin began as a joke, but the fun mascot and friendly image caught the internet's love making it widely recognized. All these altcoins try to improve on, or take a playful twist with the basic idea of digital money.

Today, altcoins are grouped into several main types, each with a special purpose or function.

### *Utility Tokens*

Utility tokens are like special keys that unlock access to a network or technology. They are not only meant to represent value but also to power the systems built on top of blockchain. ETH (Ether), which runs the Ethereum network, is a utility token because users need ETH to pay fees when running smart contracts or moving assets around. Uniswap, a service for swapping tokens, relies on the same system. Instead of being simple payment coins, utility tokens enable apps and transactions that wouldn't work otherwise. Owning them is practical. You need them to use the network's services.

### *Stablecoins*

Stablecoins pair the power of crypto with the predictability of traditional money. They are built for stability and convenience. These coins are usually tied to the value of a real-world asset, like the US dollar, so their price does not swing up and down like other cryptocurrencies. USD Coin (USDC) and Tether (USDT) are two big names in this category. People use stablecoins to move money across borders, settle trades, or protect their investments from price jumps. In daily use, you could consider stablecoins to be a digital version of cash that sits safely in your crypto wallet.

### *Meme Coins*

Meme coins are crypto projects that start as jokes or online gags but sometimes grow huge because of community excitement. Dogecoin is the famous example. It was created in minutes, all for fun, and uses the Shiba Inu dog from an old internet meme as its mascot. Even without deep technical roots, meme coins can go viral, drawing crowds and attention. Yet, what makes them captivating is not their technology but the energy and unpredictability of their online fans. They often attract speculators who hope for big swings in value.

### *Privacy Coins*

Privacy coins do what their name suggests: they shield the details of crypto transactions from public view. This focus on confidentiality can appeal to people who want to keep their financial moves private or live in places where digital freedom is threatened. Monero is a leading privacy coin, using special technology to hide both senders and amounts. Transactions on the Monero network cannot be traced like ones on Bitcoin or Ethereum. These coins offer a strong level of anonymity not found in most traditional payment systems.

Some altcoins are built for lasting value, supported by large teams, active communities, and real tools that people need. Others emerge and disappear primarily due to the influence of hype, rumors, jokes, or innovative ideas. Take Ethereum, for example: it powers NFT markets, decentralized finance apps, and whole networks of business activity. People use it every day to do things that are not possible with Bitcoin alone. On the other hand, a meme coin might rise in price just because of a social media event or celebrity tweet, with little behind it except for attention. While these coins can make headlines, their prices often swing wildly, and they rarely offer long-term solutions or uses beyond speculation.

To make the first steps into crypto investing, it helps to know what a coin actually does and who is building it. Coins with real software, well-managed teams, and active user groups are more likely to stick around. Meme coins and hot new tokens may be exciting, but they hold bigger risks. Some coins stand out for their technology or long-term vision, while others attract attention with bold promises or viral memes. For anyone interested in making their first investment, understanding what to look for becomes essential.

## Evaluating and Identifying Promising Altcoins Safely

A clear process helps separate serious projects from the rest, but no single shortcut can cut through the altcoin hype. If you've learned to spot coins with empty buzzwords or those promising wild overnight riches, you're already moving in the right direction. The next step is putting practical steps into action, breaking down coins piece by piece to judge their real worth and risks.

### *Use Case: Understanding Real Purpose*

Every altcoin should have a clear reason to exist. A strong coin usually solves a real problem, such as powering decentralized finance apps, speeding up international payments, or making online identities safer. If a project can't explain its purpose in simple terms, that's a sign to look closer.

Picture two coins: One supports a peer-to-peer lending app, showing how it helps users connect and borrow almost instantly, lowering fees and giving wider access. The other admits its only goal is to "go to the moon", a favorite meme phrase among joke coins. The first coin points to real-world use, while the second hides behind hype.

Ask questions like: Does this token unlock extra features in a service? Can it be used to pay for something, or does it only exist for trading? If answers are vague, or if the white paper feels padded with jargon and little substance, caution is warranted.

### *Team Assessment: Who's Behind the Coin?*

Checking the team is like learning the chefs behind a new restaurant before you eat there. Great coins are built by transparent groups with proven records. Start by searching for developer or company profiles on the official website. Reputable teams list members by name, link to their social profiles, and often talk openly on platforms like Twitter, Discord, or Telegram.

Scan for clear project roadmaps. Honest projects lay out their future steps, what new features will drop, when updates will happen, and how security will improve. When a coin shares regular announcements, public meetings, or developer blogs, it's a strong reassurance.

On the flip side, if the website only mentions "expert developers," shows no photos, or uses first names only, ask yourself why. Anonymous creators, no matter how compelling their claims, raise risk.

### *Market Capitalization and Liquidity*

Market capitalization is the total value of a coin's supply, calculated by multiplying the price by the number of coins in circulation. A high market cap often means a coin is more stable, and usually less likely to drop massively in value overnight. Bitcoin and Ethereum are leaders largely due to their size and trading volume.

Liquidity is just as crucial. It describes how easily you can buy or sell coins at a fair price. If there's little trading going on, you might be stuck holding coins no one else wants. Use platforms like CoinMarketCap to check daily trading volumes. If a coin has $50,000 traded each day and you want to sell $10,000, you're probably safe. If only $1,000 changes hands daily, it could be hard to exit your investment when you need to.

### *Adoption and Community Activity*

A healthy coin shows steady growth and community involvement. Look for active development on code hosting sites like GitHub. Frequent software updates and open discussion among developers signal the project is alive and kicking. Strong social media engagement, clear announcements, and fast responses to user questions give even more assurance.

Watch for signals beyond numbers—partnerships with popular wallets, integrations with business platforms, or real usage statistics bolster confidence.

### Signs of Growth

- Ongoing GitHub commits and updates
- Responsive and honest communication with users
- Partnerships or pilot programs with trusted companies
- Events, contests, and regular feedback opportunities

## *Recognizing Red Flags and Dangers*

### Rug Pulls

A "rug pull" happens when creators abandon a project after attracting large sums of money, often by yanking funds from the liquidity pool and leaving investors with worthless coins. Imagine a scenario: a new coin appears, hyped by influencers, prices skyrocket, and overnight the team's social channels go quiet. The coin's trading volume drops to almost nothing.

**Patterns to watch out for:**

- Hidden, anonymous, or unverified creators
- Smart contracts that haven't been audited or explained in public
- Claims of guaranteed massive returns
- Rushed launches without clear plans or documentation

### Other Red Flags

Be alert if you notice:

- Vague, copy-and-pasted white papers
- Minimal communication from developers
- Reviewers flagging "locked" or unfairly distributed tokens
- Shocking price jumps caused by memes or viral tweets, not by updates or business wins

## *Practical Safety Strategies*

Take cautious first steps by testing coins with small investments. Always use exchanges with a solid reputation for security and clear withdrawal processes. Double-check web addresses, bookmark official accounts, and follow reviews by trusted voices in crypto. Research using tools like CoinMarketCap for statistics or Etherscan to review smart contracts and token histories for transparency. Investing a little more time upfront can prevent future headaches and financial losses.

Now that you understand what altcoins are, their different types, and how to carefully evaluate them, you're better equipped to navigate the exciting but sometimes confusing world of crypto. By focusing on coins with real purpose, strong teams, clear plans, and active communities, and by spotting warning signs early, you can make smarter choices that protect your investments from hype and scams. Remember, taking small, thoughtful steps rather than rushing in will build your confidence and help you discover digital assets that truly add value. With this foundation, you're ready to explore altcoins more safely and begin your journey toward informed, successful crypto investing.

# CHAPTER 4
# NFTS AND THE RISE OF DIGITAL OWNERSHIP

Imagine a world where owning a unique digital item is as straightforward and secure as holding a signed piece of art in your hands. This is the promise behind NFTs, or non-fungible tokens, a new form of digital ownership that's capturing headlines and opening fresh possibilities across art, gaming, and beyond. Unlike traditional money or cryptocurrencies, NFTs represent one-of-a-kind digital assets whose authenticity and ownership are recorded on a public blockchain, making forgery nearly impossible and ownership transparent.

In this chapter, we'll break down what NFTs really are, why they've gained so much attention, and how they work behind the scenes. You'll learn about their growing role in creative industries, gaming, and even digital identity, along with practical ways to evaluate NFTs if you're considering an investment. Whether you're curious about buying your first NFT or want to understand the risks and rewards of this new digital frontier, this chapter offers clear, accessible guidance to help you navigate the landscape with confidence.

## Understanding NFTs: Definition, Popularity, and Crypto Context

Non-fungible tokens, also known as NFTs, provide a unique method to own digital assets. It helps to picture an NFT as a digital certificate of authenticity that proves a digital item is yours. While Bitcoin, dollars, or arcade tokens are interchangeable with each other, NFTs are not. For example, if you trade one dollar for another, you still have the same thing. An NFT works more like owning the signed original of a famous poster, while other people might have regular printouts or photos of that same poster.

What sets NFTs apart is their connection to the blockchain. The blockchain is like a public, tamper-proof record book that keeps track of who owns what, so you can't just copy and claim ownership of someone else's NFT. Each NFT has a unique digital signature, which can't be swapped exactly for another. This means an artist can publish a digital artwork as an NFT, and whoever buys it has the "official" copy. The NFT itself sits on the blockchain, while the image or video might be viewed by anyone, but only the NFT owner has blockchain-verified proof of ownership.

Many people get confused and think buying an NFT means you own the picture or video completely, like holding all the legal rights or stopping others from viewing it. That's not exactly true. If you buy a rare digital basketball trading card as an NFT, you might be able to display it or sell it, but you don't usually get the copyright or the right to prevent anyone else from looking at a screenshot of it online. Owning a signed comic book is akin to possessing a valuable original. While anyone can view pictures of it, only you possess the evidence that yours is the genuine item. An NFT is not the artwork itself. It's the digital proof of who owns the record of a specific version of that artwork on the blockchain.

Another big myth is that NFTs can be easily copied or faked. While you can copy the image or file, you can't clone the proof of ownership on the blockchain. The blockchain acts like a global notary office that everyone can check. If someone tries to sell a fake, the real NFT always points to the original record, making forgeries easy to spot. Some also imagine NFTs are just cryptocurrency or that they can be spent like Bitcoin or Ethereum. That's not the case. Cryptocurrencies are digital cash that can be sent, received, or spent, and each coin or token is the same. NFTs are unique items that run on some of the same technology, but they aren't spendable coins.

NFTs exploded in popularity for a mix of reasons. Celebrities and musicians began selling limited-edition songs and artwork as NFTs, which shot some headlines into the mainstream. In March 2021, a piece of digital art sold for $69 million, helping fuel worldwide interest. Video game companies let players trade NFT-based in-game items, like rare skins or weapons that you truly own, even outside the game. Sports fans started buying digital trading cards as NFTs. It also opened up a fresh path for artists and creators to earn money directly from fans, without sharing profits with big companies or galleries.

NFTs work using a process called "minting." To mint an NFT is to create a new, unique record on a blockchain. Most NFTs are minted on the Ethereum blockchain, but other blockchains support NFTs, too. After minting, the NFT exists as a digital token you can hold in a digital wallet. Think of this wallet like an app on your phone for your digital keys and assets. Smart contracts are short programs on the blockchain that manage these NFT transactions and guarantee you receive ownership, the seller gets paid, and even creators get a cut each time the NFT is resold. For example, somebody buying their first NFT might visit a marketplace, connect their wallet, pick a digital artwork, pay with cryptocurrency, and instantly get ownership recorded for them on the blockchain.

NFTs live alongside regular cryptocurrencies but fill a different role. Bitcoin and Ethereum are used for payment and as a kind of store of value, more like digital gold. NFTs use a similar "ledger" to record ownership but what you own is a specific digital thing, not a chunk of digital money. Both NFTs and cryptocurrencies require a wallet, can be bought and sold on digital marketplaces, and often live within the bigger world of decentralized apps, like DeFi lending platforms or new social networks.

Some NFTs are more than just collectibles or art. They play a role in new digital experiences like gaming, concert access, or proving your digital identity. As the uses keep expanding, NFTs are finding their way into new online adventures, which brings up questions about how they're used, how valuable they might be, and what risks come along with them. That's where the journey continues into the practical ways NFTs shape digital ownership, work as investments, and show up across industries beyond art and collectibles.

## NFT Applications and Critical Evaluation for Investors

Walking through the expanding uses of NFTs unveils a world that blends creativity, identity, and social connection with a brand-new type of ownership. One of the first fields where NFTs made headlines was digital art. Artists who once struggled to earn a living online are now selling their work directly to fans as digital originals. Each NFT links to a single, unique piece of art stored and verified on a blockchain, like a digital signature proving both authenticity and ownership. For example, when Beeple sold his piece "Everydays: The First 5000 Days" as an NFT, it fetched millions and showed how digital artwork could be collected and traded with the same pride as a painting in a gallery. Collectors now browse platforms such as OpenSea, Rarible, or Foundation to discover works that come with verifiable histories and the sense of being the only official version in the world. But buying digital art also brings risks: images can be copied, artists may not always receive royalties, and high-profile sales attract imitators hoping to cash in.

NFTs have transformed gaming with a more interactive kind of ownership. In traditional games, players buy skins, weapons, or characters, but those items usually belong to the game company, not to the player. NFT-powered games flip that model. Assets such as swords, rare costumes, or even whole virtual land plots are minted as NFTs, which players can buy, sell, or trade as they wish. A positive example is Axie Infinity, a game where players breed, trade, and battle digital pets called Axies. Each Axie is an NFT on the blockchain, with its traits and value determined by rarity and demand. Players can earn, trade, or even lend their NFTs within the gaming community. This structure provides significant value to the time and money invested in the game, yet it presents both advantages and disadvantages. High upfront costs make some NFT games pay-to-play, and the market for in-game items can become a bubble, forcing latecomers to pay more for the same digital goods.

NFTs also play a growing role in digital identity and credentials. Rather than relying on usernames and passwords, people can use blockchain-powered certificates that prove who they are or what skills they've earned. For instance, a university might issue a diploma as an NFT, allowing employers to directly verify its origin and authenticity. Musicians and artists can launch membership passes as NFTs, granting owners exclusive access to live events, digital meet-ups, or special content. These tokens work like digital keys; if you own the right one, you're invited. This model is catching on with brands and content creators who want to reward loyal fans with early access or exclusive merchandise.

As NFT ownership expands, the investment question moves to the front of many minds. Some readers might wonder whether NFTs are the next big asset class, like Bitcoin or stocks. NFT markets have seen gigantic price swings. Some early buyers sold cartoon images or short clips for hundreds or thousands of times their purchase price. Yet prices can crash just as quickly, leaving others with assets they can't resell. A market full of excitement draws scammers and low-quality projects, making it challenging to pick a winner. Stories abound; some win life-changing profits by grabbing rare items early, while many more sink money into tokens that never sell again. The most successful NFTs tend to offer not only scarcity and eye-catching art but also strong communities, clear practical uses, and backing by recognizable artists or brands. Even then, holding an NFT doesn't always mean you own the copyright or that you're protected from copycats.

Anyone thinking about buying or investing in NFTs should practice solid critical thinking and avoid buying based on hype. Here are important questions to ask before hitting "buy":

- Who is the creator or team behind the NFT? Do they have a reliable track record?
- What does the NFT offer the owner beyond the digital image or code? Does it include real-world perks, access, or future collaborations?
- Is the token rare, or will lots more be created, diluting its value?
- How active and supportive is the community around the project? Are other owners excited, engaged, and helping the project grow, or does it look abandoned?
- How easy is it to resell the NFT if you change your mind? Are there enough buyers, or is the market thin?
- Is the platform safe, and does it have protections against scams or sudden shutdowns?
- What rights do you actually receive? Owning the NFT doesn't always mean owning commercial rights to the artwork or using the asset however you want.

Looking past the headlines means checking real utility, active communities, proven creators, and platforms with a history of safe transactions. If an offer appears excessively favorable or appears hasty, it typically indicates a need to take a more measured approach. The best approach blends curiosity with healthy skepticism, aiming not for quick wins but for solid, informed decisions anchored in real value and lasting impact.

Now that we understand what NFTs are, why they matter, and how to evaluate them carefully, you're better equipped to navigate this fast-changing digital landscape with confidence. NFTs offer exciting possibilities, from owning unique art and in-game items to proving your identity and accessing exclusive experiences, but they also come with risks and complexities that demand thoughtful attention. By focusing on real value, trustworthy creators, and clear benefits rather than hype or quick profits, you can make smarter choices and avoid common pitfalls. As NFTs continue to grow and evolve, keeping a cautious but curious mindset will help you seize opportunities while protecting your investments in this new era of digital ownership.

# CHAPTER 5

# HOW TO BUY YOUR FIRST CRYPTO (STEP-BY-STEP)

"When I bought my first Bitcoin, I felt completely lost, like I had stumbled into a foreign country without a map," said one new investor. That feeling is common. The world of cryptocurrency can seem complicated and risky, especially for those who haven't dived into digital finance before. It's easy to worry about making mistakes or falling for scams when every step involves dealing with unfamiliar terms and websites. Yet, buying your first crypto doesn't have to be confusing or scary. With the right guidance, anyone can take this first step safely and confidently. This chapter offers practical insight designed just for beginners like you, helping you choose the right place to start, set up your account securely, and move forward with clarity rather than fear.

## Selecting an Exchange and Creating Your Account

Cryptocurrency exchanges are the websites and apps that make it possible to buy, sell, and store digital currencies such as

Bitcoin or Ethereum. Think of them as the digital shops where your crypto journey begins. Every beginner's first step is picking one of these "shops," and that choice matters for one clear reason: not all exchanges are equally safe, simple to use, or trustworthy. A solid platform protects your money and simplifies the learning process.

Some global exchanges you'll see mentioned often include Coinbase, Binance, and Kraken. These names have earned trust over years of operation, strict rules, and serving millions of users. Differences crop up when comparing them to smaller or offshore exchanges, which might have lighter regulation or be more vulnerable to hacks or sudden shutdowns. Highly regulated exchanges follow rules set by government bodies in places like the US or Europe. They offer a safety net for beginners because the law requires basic security and fair business practices.

Before making an account, you want to compare and check off a few must-have features for your own peace of mind.

## *What to Look For in a Good Exchange*

### Security

- Two-factor authentication (2FA) so you need a password *and* a code from your phone to log in or move funds
- Withdrawal whitelist features, letting you choose trusted wallet addresses and blocking others from draining your account

- Cold storage for customer money; most trusted exchanges keep most funds offline where hackers can't reach
- Solid track record with no major hacks or prompt, public reimbursement after any incident

A risky exchange lacks these features, uses only passwords, has been hacked with customer losses, or hides security details. On the other hand, a platform like Coinbase shows clear guides on enabling 2FA, describes insurance policies, and announces upgrades against new threats.

### Reputation

- Look for industry awards, positive user reviews, and press coverage in major outlets
- Regulatory registration and a clear company history you can double-check
- No scandals, shutdowns, or reports of missing funds in the news or user forums

Imagine finding "Best Crypto Platform for Beginners" badges, a strong review score, and recent news articles describing steady growth. Compare that to an exchange with no press, angry comments, or a missing "about us" page.

### Beginner-Friendliness

- Easy sign-up and clear navigation (large buttons, step-by-step help, transparent menus)
- Demo or "practice," modes for learning without risking money
- Chat or email support for new users guarantees a response within hours.
- Help sections should use simple language instead of confusing technical terms.

Popular exchanges often offer pop-up guides and even 24/7 chat teams, so getting stuck is rare.

To organize your choice, create a shortlist of three exchanges. Number them based on which seems safest and easiest after comparing criteria above. Double-check their features, reviews, and support before deciding which one to use.

## *How to Create Your Account, Step-by-Step*

1. Open a browser or the app store and search for the exchange you chose. Make sure the URL starts with "https://" and shows a padlock icon. The padlock proves the website is secure.

Never click on links from emails or social media ads to avoid fake copycat websites.

2. Tap "Sign Up" and fill in your email and a *strong, unique* password. Never use old passwords reused anywhere else.

**Weak:** password123

**Strong:** Bx7$2mp9!cYE4qWz

Write your password down on paper or use a password manager.

3. After entering your email, check your inbox for a new message from the exchange. Click the link or enter the code sent to you. This step proves it's really you signing up.
4. The platform will guide you to upload documents for verification—a driver's license or passport photo, and maybe a quick selfie taken with your camera. This is required by law in many countries to prevent money laundering. Expect to wait a few minutes (or sometimes longer) while they confirm your ID. Double-check all your info matches exactly what's on your documents.
5. Once verified, set up two-factor authentication by linking your phone number or scanning a QR code with an authenticator app. Always enable this setting. It prevents anyone from logging in without your device.

Check every step before you hit "Submit." Turn on malware protection on your device and avoid doing this over public Wi-Fi.

### *Encouragement for Small Purchases*

Many new investors start with $50 or even less. Every major exchange allows purchases as low as $1 to $10. This is a smart way to learn without overstretching. When you first log in, you may see a message like "Minimum first purchase: $5." It's normal, not a trick, and lets you get comfortable before making larger moves.

Completing registration and securing your account opens the door to your first buy. The steps you've just finished unlock every tool and setting you'll use to purchase crypto safely. Up next, you'll learn exactly how to fund your account and make your first investment with confidence.

## Making Your First Purchase and Managing Security Settings

You have set up your exchange account and finished verification. The next steps bring you right to the heart of crypto: buying your first coins. When you log into your chosen exchange, focus on finding the area where purchases happen. The layout will look different depending on which exchange you use, but some patterns show up everywhere. On Coinbase, a blue "Buy/Sell" button sits on the top bar; this is your entry point. Binance has a "Buy Crypto" button right on the homepage, while Kraken's "Buy Crypto" link appears in the navigation menu. Look in the top menu, sidebar, or main dashboard for words like "Buy," "Trade," or "Markets." These are your signposts. If you don't see anything jumping out, try expanding the main dashboard menu since some platforms group all trading features together.

Once you enter the buy or trade screen, the exchange usually asks which cryptocurrency you want to buy. You might see a long list, a drop-down menu, or a search box. There are hundreds of coins out there, some with suspiciously similar names. Only buy large, reputable assets for your first purchase. For example, if you want Bitcoin, look for its official symbol, BTC. Ethereum is always ETH. Beware of coins with extra letters or odd punctuation - "BitcoinCash" is BCH (different from BTC), and "Ethereum Classic" is ETC (not ETH). If in doubt, check the exchange's information card, which almost always displays the coin's name and ticker symbol together.

Most exchanges make it easy to search. Start typing "Bitcoin" or "BTC" in the buy screen. The correct result usually pops up at the top, but always pause a second to look at the details. Stick with coins listed on the platform's main screen, as these go through a review before being offered. If you see a warning, low liquidity badge, or exclamation point, skip those for now.

After choosing your coin, the next step is deciding how much to buy. A simple field allows you to type in an amount in dollars or another local currency, or sometimes in the coin itself, such as 0.01 BTC. For beginners, start with a small, affordable amount that helps you get comfortable. You may see options for "Market Price" or "Limit Order." "Market Price" lets you buy instantly at the current rate, while a "Limit Order" allows you to set a preferred price and wait for the market to reach it. Limit orders can be confusing at first and are not necessary for your initial purchase, so stick with the market or instant option if available. If you see fields for payment methods or destination wallets, make sure the correct account or card is selected. Some platforms default to bank transfers, while others use linked debit cards.

Before confirming the purchase, you'll see a review screen. Exchanges typically display fees clearly, either as a dollar amount or a percentage. For example, on Coinbase, a $100 purchase may include a $2.99 fee, giving you about $97 worth of crypto. Most exchanges show this breakdown beneath your total. You will also notice purchase limits, since many platforms prevent you from buying less than a certain amount, such as $10, or more than your verified status allows. Avoid spending your entire balance on your first attempt, as digital coins can be volatile. A small purchase keeps the process low-pressure and helps you learn without stress.

Security is your lifeline. Enable two-factor authentication (2FA) before or immediately after your first purchase. This adds an extra layer of protection by combining your password with a code from your phone app or a text message. For instance, if someone steals your password, 2FA still prevents them from accessing your account. Never reuse old or simple passwords. Choose strong, unique ones that are not used elsewhere, and always use secure devices instead of public Wi-Fi.

After you click "Buy," you'll usually see a summary screen with your transaction details. The cryptocurrency amount may appear in your balance right away, especially for market orders, but sometimes the status shows "pending" while the payment clears. Some exchanges send an email receipt or a pop-up confirmation. Payments made by card tend to process faster than bank transfers, which can take a few hours or even longer for first-time buyers. If your crypto doesn't appear immediately, stay calm. Most delays last only a few minutes or a couple of hours, rarely more.

If something doesn't go as planned, you're not alone. A declined card, slow payment, or failed identity check can happen. Double-check your payment information, try a different card, or complete any verification steps in your profile. Minor issues, such as a "pending" status that lasts a bit longer than expected, rarely mean a loss. Contact customer support only if the delay continues or if an error message won't clear. Most exchanges want your business and are quick to resolve issues. Patience, along with steady, deliberate actions, keeps you in control.

Now that you've learned how to choose a trustworthy exchange and secure your account, you're ready to move forward with confidence. By taking practical steps like selecting a reliable platform, enabling strong security features, and starting with small purchases, you've built a solid foundation for your crypto journey. This careful approach helps you avoid common pitfalls and gives you full control. In the chapters ahead, you'll explore how to fund your account, make your first purchase, and manage your investments safely, all while deepening your understanding of this fast-evolving world without unnecessary risk or confusion.

# CHAPTER 6
# STORING YOUR CRYPTO SAFELY – WALLETS 101

More than 20% of all Bitcoin in existence has been lost or become inaccessible, often because people didn't take the right steps to protect their digital wallets. Unlike traditional money kept in banks, cryptocurrency exists entirely online, making it vulnerable to hackers, scams, and simple mistakes. Many new investors don't realize that where and how they store their crypto is just as important as buying it. Losing access to your funds isn't a matter of if, but when, unless you know how to keep them safe. This chapter will help you understand why securing your crypto matters and introduce the tools and methods that place control firmly in your hands.

## Understanding Exchange Risks and Types of Crypto Wallets

Buying crypto is only the first step. Where you keep it determines whether you're truly in control of your money or exposed to outside risks. When coins remain on exchanges, the same platforms where you bought them, you give someone else power over your funds. It feels easy and familiar, like leaving your paychecks in a checking account. However, with crypto, exchanges can be surprisingly fragile.

Major exchanges have faced headline-making disasters that shattered trust across the industry. Consider the Mt. Gox collapse, where more than 800,000 Bitcoin disappeared overnight, leaving thousands of people locked out of their assets permanently. The Canadian platform QuadrigaCX met a similar fate when its founder died suddenly, and users soon discovered that hundreds of millions in coins were gone for good. These events may sound sensational, but they all stem from one problem: the risk of storing digital wealth in places beyond your control.

The key lesson is simple: "not your keys, not your coins." Imagine owning a house but giving the only key to a stranger. Every time you want to enter, you must wait for them to unlock the door. If something happens to them, or they choose to walk away, you lose access completely, no matter how much you trust them. Leaving crypto on exchanges requires a similar act of blind trust.

Take control of your security by understanding how crypto wallets work. A wallet in crypto isn't a place where coins physically sit. Instead, it's a digital tool that stores the credentials needed to access and move your funds on the blockchain. When you hold your own private keys, you are the only person who can decide how to use your assets. Every wallet allows you to receive, store, and send coins, but they fall into two main categories: hot and cold.

Hot wallets are software-based and connected to the internet. They come as browser extensions, phone apps, or desktop programs. They are quick and simple to set up, which makes them popular for beginners and everyday transactions. Apps such as MetaMask and Trust Wallet let you create a wallet and start sending or receiving crypto within minutes. The main advantage is convenience. If you use small amounts of crypto for regular purchases, a hot wallet functions like the wallet in your pocket, ready for coffee runs, online shopping, or small payments.

But being always connected to the internet is double-edged. Hot wallets are vulnerable to phishing, viruses, or hackers getting into your phone or computer. The same speed that makes these tools useful for fast access also poses a risk to users who store all their information online.

Ready for a sturdier option? Hardware wallets, also known as cold wallets, remain offline unless you choose to connect them. Devices such as Ledger Nano S, Ledger Nano X, and Trezor look like USB drives or small gadgets with screens. When you set one up, your private keys are created and stored securely inside the device. Only when you connect it to your computer to approve a transaction does your wallet interact with the internet, and even then, your private data never leaves the hardware. Think of a cold wallet as a safe deposit box at the bank. You use it to store your valuables long-term and only access them when you want to move a large amount.

Comparing the two makes the trade-offs clear. Hot wallets make spending easy but carry more day-to-day risk if you hold significant sums. Cold wallets provide stronger protection and peace of mind for long-term storage but are less convenient for frequent transactions.

Several misconceptions can trip up beginners. Some people believe all wallets offer the same level of security, but that is not true. Leaving your entire investment in a hot wallet or on an exchange creates open doors for thieves. On the other hand, hardware devices may look intimidating, but setting them up is straightforward and requires no advanced technical skills. Most popular hardware wallets guide you through the process with clear screens and step-by-step instructions. Think of it like buying a fireproof safe. You do not need to be a locksmith. You simply follow basic setup steps, record your backup code securely, and your valuables are protected.

Start by considering your habits and your comfort with risk. If you hold a small amount of crypto that you use regularly, a hot wallet is practical. For larger balances or assets you plan to hold long-term, dividing your funds between hot and cold storage is the safest approach. Keep only what you need for daily spending in a hot wallet, and store the rest securely in a hardware device.

Once you understand the basic types and what makes them safe, the next question is: how do you pick the right wallet and avoid mistakes that could lose your funds? You'll want to know how to create backups, where and how to hide your recovery phrases, and ways to spot fake software. These first steps pave the way for securing your crypto with real confidence, never relying on luck or hope alone.

## Choosing the Right Wallet and Protecting Your Assets

Understanding the differences between hot and cold wallets sets the stage for what really matters: making sure your crypto stays safe as you use it day by day. After learning about storage types, the next real question is what fits your needs and routines. Security isn't just an abstract worry. Once you hold digital assets, even small amounts, your focus shifts to practical control, seeing your assets available but protected from theft, mistakes, or gadget failures.

### *Matching Wallets to Real-Life Habits*

A wallet is not a universally applicable tool. Your ideal choice depends on how you use your crypto. If you want a simple way to access and manage tokens for daily use, you may lean toward an app or browser extension. If your main focus is security and you plan to hold rather than trade often, physical devices make more sense.

#### MetaMask

MetaMask is a software wallet that works as a browser extension or mobile app. It's a favorite for new users who want to interact with decentralized apps or buy, store, and send Ethereum and similar tokens. Setting up MetaMask begins with a simple app installation. Once inside, friendly prompts and visual cues guide you. You'll see current balances, recent transactions, and ways to connect to trading sites or apps, all in one place.

For someone buying crypto for the first time, MetaMask can hold small amounts for regular use, like buying an NFT or swapping coins. The main draw is ease: install, follow the prompts, and you're ready to interact. Still, MetaMask's convenience means your assets are only as safe as your device. If you use MetaMask on a laptop or phone, malware or theft can reach your wallet unless you take extra care.

### Ledger

Ledger is a hardware wallet, a physical device that stores your private keys offline. The most popular models look like small USB drives. To set it up, you connect it to a computer, walk through step-by-step screens, and write down a recovery phrase. Ledger's real advantage is security. Since your keys never touch the internet, they stay protected from hackers, even if your computer is infected.

For those building a crypto nest egg or holding coins for months or years, Ledger shifts control to you. Think of it like a home safe: no one can access it unless they hold the device and the recovery phrase. There is a learning curve, plugging in, using the app, and following instructions to approve each action, but it becomes routine with practice. Someone holding Bitcoin for the long haul may move large amounts to Ledger for peace of mind and only remove assets when needed.

### Trust Wallet

Trust Wallet is a mobile app tailored for broad crypto support. It allows users to buy, store, swap, and stake a wide range of coins from their phone. Beginners find Trust Wallet friendly due to its clean interface and strong cheat sheets guiding setup. Imagine a person on the go, wanting to manage collectibles, sign into games, or keep daily spending money handy; Trust Wallet offers that flexibility.

Compared with MetaMask or Ledger, Trust Wallet sits in the middle. It's more secure than a browser alone but not as protected as a device kept offline. The main tradeoff is between ease of access and the risk if your phone is lost or breached.

### *Protective Habits for All Wallets*

Choosing a wallet is step one. Keeping it safe makes all the difference. Start with creating secure passwords for every app and device, using a mix of random letters, numbers, and symbols. Never use names, birthdays, or words someone could guess. If your wallet app offers two-factor authentication (2FA), always enable it. 2FA asks for a code from your phone or another app when signing in, blocking intruders even if they steal your password.

Next, generate and save your seed phrase, 12 or 24 random words that unlock your wallet from any device. Write these down on paper, not on your phone, not in emails, and never in cloud storage. Some people make the mistake of screenshotting their phrase or sending it to themselves via chat. This exposes funds to anyone who hacks the account. Instead, keep the paper hidden somewhere only you can reach.

Backup matters too. Store wallet details and recovery phrases in a secure box or safe. Tell only one trusted person where this backup exists, in case of accidents. Never type private keys or seed phrases into unknown websites or support chat windows. Only enter them during wallet setup, and only through the official app or device.

Take a moment before using any wallet app. Check you're using the real one, not a fake. On hardware wallets, verify the device is genuine and behaves as expected. Scammers use fake apps and phishing to steal coins.

Losing a device doesn't mean losing assets if you have your seed phrase. You can restore your wallet on a new phone or hardware device using the backup. Without those recovery words, even the company behind the wallet cannot get your funds back. Treat this information like your own digital bank vault.

Making these safety measures habits reduces anxiety and puts you firmly in control. Handling crypto gets smoother when you build security into your daily life. Each step, from choosing a wallet to storing backup phrases, fits into a pattern of awareness and care that anyone can learn.

Now that you understand the critical importance of securely storing your cryptocurrency and the practical ways to protect your assets, you're ready to take control with confidence. Whether you choose a hot wallet for everyday convenience or a cold wallet for long-term safety, the key is matching your tools to your habits and risk level. By adopting good security practices, like safeguarding your seed phrase, using strong passwords, and verifying your wallet apps, you can avoid common pitfalls and keep your digital wealth truly yours. With these foundations in place, you're prepared to navigate the crypto world safely, turning curiosity into smart, secure investing.

# CHAPTER 7
# HOW TO BUILD A SMART, SIMPLE CRYPTO PORTFOLIO

Emma clicked through her crypto wallet, heart pounding as she stared at dozens of coins she'd bought over the past few months. Each one promised huge returns—tweets, forums, and flashy headlines had pulled her deeper into a world she barely understood. Yet instead of feeling excited, she felt overwhelmed, confused by the sheer number of assets and news to track. Every day seemed like a gamble, and the fear of missing out pushed her to buy more, even when she didn't fully grasp what she owned.

If you've ever found yourself in Emma's shoes, wondering how to balance hope for growth with caution, you're not alone. Many new investors jump in thinking success means owning every popular coin or chasing the next big thing. But that approach can lead to stress, confusion, and losses, making it harder to build real confidence or steady gains.

This chapter steps back from the chaos to show how keeping your crypto portfolio smart and simple can make all the difference. You'll see why focusing on a few solid choices, not dozens, helps protect your money and your peace of mind. Whether you want slow, steady growth or are curious about reaching for bigger wins without losing sleep, there's a way to create a plan that fits your comfort level and goals.

Before investing, learn the value of simplicity and strategy in the fast-paced crypto world. This isn't about hype or rushing; it's about building a thoughtful foundation that sets you up to learn, grow, and invest smarter over time.

## Understanding Portfolio Simplicity and Sample Beginner Portfolios

Think of your crypto portfolio like a grocery basket. You wouldn't grab everything in the shop, you'd get the basics, maybe something new you've researched, and skip what feels too strange or risky. In crypto, there's a common myth that real success comes from owning a slice of everything or filling your digital wallet with as many coins as you can. The truth is, especially for someone just starting out, a few well-chosen coins bring more control, less stress, and a much safer journey.

Spreading money over too many coins turns portfolio management into a guessing game. With so many projects launching and social media hype running wild, it's easy to believe you're missing out if you're not constantly adding new tokens. But holding every new coin or trendy project means you're less likely to understand the details of what you actually own. This brings a hidden risk: some lesser-known coins can crash hard, lose value overnight, or even disappear. Chasing every opportunity often leads to more confusion and bigger losses than steady progress.

Simplicity also protects your time and peace of mind. Just as most people wouldn't buy every stock on the market, you don't need to fill your crypto portfolio with dozens of coins. The more coins you have, the more difficult it becomes to track performance, spot risks, and keep up with news and security measures for each asset. Focusing on a handful of coins means you can actually follow what's happening, learn how they behave during market swings, and make smarter decisions when it matters most.

Building around a few leading assets makes you less likely to end up with "dead weight" in your portfolio; those coins that sit forgotten, performing poorly while eating up space and money. Sticking to a simple, thoughtful mix keeps things easy to monitor. This gives you space to build confidence at your pace, without being pulled in a thousand directions.

### *Sample Beginner Portfolios by Risk Tolerance*

Pick a portfolio based on how much risk makes sense for your life and your goals. Here's what that looks like in practice, with three sample strategies:

## Conservative Portfolio

A conservative portfolio means putting most of your money into the oldest, most established coins. These assets have the longest track records and the strongest reputations for surviving price drops and market trouble. For a simple option:

- **Bitcoin:** 60%
- **Ethereum:** 35%
- **USDC (a leading stablecoin):** 5%

This is for someone like Sarah, who wants steady growth and doesn't want many surprises. She checks her account a few times a month rather than every day and likes knowing her money is in coins that the whole industry watches closely. Her goal is gradual wealth-building over several years, not quick profits.

## Balanced Portfolio

A balanced portfolio shares funds between big-name coins and a small slice of promising alternatives. It suits people who want to capture more upside but prefer to keep most of their money in safer bets. An example split:

- **Bitcoin:** 50%
- **Ethereum:** 30%
- **Cardano or Solana:** 15%
- **USDC:** 5%

Imagine Justin, who's curious enough to research new technologies but still needs stability. He's comfortable reading up on news about his top coins and likes having one pick outside the top two for new growth. His ambition is to grow his money faster than a savings account while avoiding the high drama of riskier portfolios.

### Aggressive Portfolio

An aggressive portfolio leans hard into emerging coins with the hope of higher returns and accepts the swings that come with that. Here's a setup for the bold:

- **Bitcoin:** 40%
- **Ethereum:** 25%
- **Solana:** 10%
- **Polygon:** 10%
- **Small-Cap Coin:** 10%
- **USDC:** 5%

Jenny, for instance, wants a shot at bigger gains and likes hunting for the next breakout star. She spends time researching new crypto projects, follows developers on social media, and is fine with value jumping up and down. What drives her is potential upside, but she understands this brings periods of losses along the way.

### *Matching Your Approach*

The best fit depends on how hands-on you want to be and how much you can handle watching prices move around. Ask yourself:

- Do I want quiet, long-term growth or the chance for faster wins and losses?
- Am I willing to spend time keeping up with new projects and news?
- Will big swings in value make me anxious, or are they part of the thrill?

Pick a structure that leaves you sleeping well at night, not staring at charts at 2 a.m. Don't copy someone else's choices. Your mix should match your personal feeling about risk, time, and learning style.

Now that you've seen what a focused portfolio looks like, the big questions become about how to split your money, balance coins, and keep things working over time. This is where strategy comes to life, and your blueprint for safe, practical investing really begins to take shape.

## Allocating, Diversifying, and Maintaining Your Crypto Portfolio

Building on earlier portfolio templates, it's time to turn those ideas into reality. Many new investors think success means owning dozens of coins, but picking just a few solid choices and sticking to a clear plan can be safer and less stressful. Three big skills - allocation, diversification, and rebalancing make those plans easier to follow.

### *Allocation: How much should I put where?*

Allocation means deciding how much money you'll put into each crypto asset. Instead of jumping in and buying whatever looks hot, you take your total investment amount and make a careful plan. Let's say you have $1,000 saved for this goal. You might decide on a split like

- 60% Bitcoin (BTC) = $600
- 30% Ethereum (ETH) = $300
- 10% Solana (SOL) = $100

A safer, lower-risk style might use 80% in BTC, 15% in ETH, and only 5% in an altcoin. Risk-tolerant investors might go the other way, but beginners should remember: more money in the older, bigger coins gives you a cushion if prices swing.

Why think about allocation so seriously? Writing down your plan helps you avoid the urge to chase big winners or dump everything when prices fall. Those clear boundaries make it less likely you'll panic during the next market dip. Whenever you add more money to your portfolio, use your chosen percentages again to keep things simple.

### *Diversification: Don't put all your eggs in one basket*

Diversification protects you from the risk that one coin performs badly while another does well. Instead of betting on a single asset, you spread your investment over several. For example, suppose your portfolio is 100% BTC. If BTC drops 40% in a few months, your entire investment falls by 40%. But if your allocation is 50% BTC, 40% ETH, and 10% SOL, and during a tough season BTC drops 40%, ETH holds steady, and SOL rises 20%, your losses are softened.

Here's a simple way to think about it:

- If one asset is down, others might be stable
- Winners and losers often take turns
- Keeping three to five coins avoids confusion
- More coins aren't always better; just one or two will pose more risk than a balanced basket

Sticking to a handful of familiar, trusted coins protects you from hype and hidden dangers. For most beginners, starting with BTC, ETH, and one or two more is both practical and smart.

### *Rebalancing: Check and adjust your plan*

Markets move, and so will the value of the assets you own. Over time, one coin might double while another drifts down.

Your portfolio could drift from your original plan. This is where rebalancing comes in. Rebalancing means checking regularly to see if your allocations still match your target percentages. If they don't, you sell some of what's grown and buy what's lagged until things are back in line.

Here's a simple checklist:

- Pick a schedule (every 3 or 6 months)
- Review your coin values and amounts
- Compare to your original percentage plan
- Sell a portion of coins that grew above target
- Buy coins that slipped below target

### Example

Suppose your target is 60% BTC, 30% ETH, 10% SOL. After three months, BTC soared to 70% of your portfolio. You'd sell part of your BTC and shift that money to ETH or SOL to restore your original balance. This routine keeps your risk level from drifting up without your noticing.

## *Dollar-Cost Averaging (DCA): A steadier approach to buying*

Dollar-cost averaging (DCA) is a process where you invest set amounts (say $100) at regular intervals (like monthly), instead of trying to guess the perfect time to buy. Some months prices will be higher, some lower, and your buying average smooths out over time.

Picture a six-month scenario:

- Month 1: $100 at $30,000 (BTC)
- Month 2: $100 at $32,000
- Month 3: $100 at $28,000
- Month 4: $100 at $25,000
- Month 5: $100 at $26,000
- Month 6: $100 at $31,000

Your average buy price comes out much lower than if you'd poured in $600 all at once during a price spike. DCA keeps you from stressing over day-to-day moves and lets you stay in the game steadily.

## *Long-term thinking: Patience beats panic*

Short-term volatility in crypto can trigger big emotional swings. When prices fall, the urge to sell and "cut losses" is strong. But history shows that most people who hold quality coins through downturns tend to recover and often come out ahead. For instance, someone who bought BTC during its all-time high in 2017 and held through the deep 2018 crash still saw the value multiply by 2021. Someone else who panicked and sold early missed out.

**illustration:**

| Year | BTC Price |
|---|---|
| 2017 | $19,000 |
| 2018 | $6,000 |

Sticking to a clear plan, rebalancing regularly, and keeping a long-term mindset can help protect your investments and your peace of mind.

Now that you understand how to build a simple, balanced cryptocurrency portfolio tailored to your comfort with risk and time, you're ready to take practical steps toward smart investing. Keeping your focus on a few well-chosen coins helps you stay in control, avoid common pitfalls, and grow your confidence as you learn more about this exciting space. By planning your allocation, diversifying thoughtfully, rebalancing regularly, and embracing patience, you create a strong foundation that can weather the ups and downs of crypto markets. With these tools in hand, you can move forward with clarity and calm, turning your curiosity into steady, informed action on your journey to building digital wealth.

CHAPTER 8

# UNDERSTANDING RISK (AND HOW TO AVOID LOSING IT ALL)

Did you know that the value of many cryptocurrencies can swing by double digits within just a few hours? Unlike traditional markets that close for the day, crypto trades nonstop, leading to rapid and often unexpected price changes. These wild ups and downs can make investing in digital currencies feel like riding a rollercoaster without a seatbelt. Understanding why these shifts happen and how emotions influence decisions is key to protecting your money. This chapter will guide you through the nature of cryptocurrency risk and offer practical ways to keep control, even when the market feels unpredictable.

## Decoding Crypto Volatility and Investor Emotions

Cryptocurrency prices can jump or crash in what feels like the blink of an eye. Unlike traditional stock markets that follow business hours, crypto trading happens every hour of every day, and anyone in the world can join in. This means prices are always moving, sometimes in big, unpredictable ways. Many of these wild swings happen because the market is still fairly new. Bitcoin, for example, only launched in 2009, so compared to stocks or gold, its "track record" is quite short. Most cryptocurrencies have even less history, leaving investors with fewer data points to feel steady about.

Another reason for big price jumps is the size of the market itself. The total value of all cryptocurrencies is much smaller than traditional financial markets. In a smaller market, even a few people moving money in or out can make a big difference in price. Picture a seesaw on a playground: if only one or two people climb on, it teeters quickly. Crypto's playground works in a similar way. Because crypto assets are traded all over the world, any big piece of news or sudden action from a large investor, sometimes called a "whale", can tip the market fast. If someone with a giant stash of bitcoin decides to sell, the whole price can drop suddenly, catching smaller investors off guard.

News stories and social media posts spark quick reactions, too. A single celebrity tweet or a government regulation announcement can send prices soaring or crashing almost instantly. For example, when a famous entrepreneur once tweeted support for Bitcoin, the price shot up in minutes. But when the same person later expressed doubts, prices dipped just as fast. In another case, when a country's government announced a possible ban on crypto, panic spread and led to a steep sell-off. These types of dramatic rises and falls are called volatility. Some people see chances to make money in these swings, but for newcomers, it often feels confusing or worrying.

There are solid ways to hold steady even when the market looks like a rollercoaster. The first trick is to decide ahead of time how much you can afford to invest and only use money you could lose without it hurting your life. This way, big price drops won't put you in real trouble. Many smart investors also spread their money across more than one kind of crypto or even keep some in regular savings, so if one coin crashes, they still have something left. Setting clear rules for when to buy or sell, rather than acting on a whim, makes panic less likely.

It helps to look at the long road, not just today's price. Crypto often bounces up and down in the short term, but steps upward and downward shape long-term trends. Some people call this approach HODLing, which means holding onto your investment even during storms. For example, an investor who bought bitcoin a few years ago might have watched its price drop by half in just a week. Some people sold everything in fear, but this person waited patiently until the price recovered and even climbed above their original buying point.

When chaos strikes, it's tempting to follow rumors or invest in the newest tip. By sticking with your original plan and ignoring daily drama, you let the odds work for you over time. A simple checklist helps: before making any move, ask yourself if this fits your plan or if you're just reacting to headlines or a friend's advice.

Emotions push people to make choices they later regret. FOMO, or "fear of missing out," happens when you see prices rising and want to buy in so you don't miss gains, even if you haven't researched the project. Greed urges people to chase quick profits, buying when prices are already high in hopes of more. Panic selling occurs when prices decline, fear overwhelms, and individuals rush to sell, often resulting in significant losses. These feelings are normal, but they can make you act against your interest.

To sidestep these emotional traps, write down your reasons for every investment. If you set a goal like selling if your coin rises 30% or only investing a set amount stick with it. When headlines start to worry you, read your journal and remember how you made those choices. By noticing your own feelings, you can stop yourself from trading impulsively and focus on steady growth.

Learning how crypto markets twist and turn, and understanding your own reactions, gives you a guidebook for calmer investing. Beyond these basics, you'll need smart ways to keep your risk low, not just to avoid losing money, but to spot trouble before it starts. The next parts will break down clear strategies for safer investing so you can act confidently no matter what the markets throw your way.

## Beginner Risk Management and Avoiding Costly Mistakes

Everyone feels the pull of excitement when crypto prices soar or a friend brags about huge gains. That buzz of possibility isn't just emotional; it can cloud judgment and put beginner investors in harm's way. One minute you're curious, the next you're feeling FOMO and hitting "buy" based on a hot tip. This emotional rollercoaster mixes with genuine complexity, creating a setting where mistakes and scams can sneak up fast. The secret is turning that anxious energy into action. Risk can't be erased, but it can be managed.

### *Practical Risk Management Techniques*

Basic steps lay the groundwork for safer investing. Security comes first. Use a strong password for every crypto account, mixing letters, numbers, and symbols, and never repeat passwords. Two-factor authentication (2FA) adds another wall between your assets and intruders. With 2FA, even if someone steals your password, they still need a code from your phone or another secure device. For the most secure storage, hardware wallets keep crypto offline, protecting it from internet hacks. These are tiny devices like USB sticks, if they're not plugged in, your assets are unreachable through cyberattacks.

Solid portfolio habits matter just as much. Never invest money you depend on for rent, groceries, or emergencies. Crypto's price swings are unpredictable, you might see deep drops within days. Instead, decide the total amount you're comfortable losing entirely, and treat that as your upper limit. Diversification means spreading your investment across several coins or tokens to avoid heavy damage if one crashes. If you buy only one currency and it tanks, your whole portfolio suffers.

Taking profits on the way up helps sidestep regret. Suppose you buy a coin for $500, it doubles, and you sell half your holdings. Even if the price falls afterward, you've already taken gains and protected your original funds. Stop-loss orders can limit disaster by selling automatically if a price dips past your chosen threshold. For example, you set a stop-loss at 15% below your buy price. If the market tumbles, your assets get sold before you lose much more.

When prices jump after you invest, resist the urge to "chase" and keep pouring in more. Hype often fades as quickly as it arrived, and newcomers can be left with big losses while earlier sellers cash out. Take time to check facts and reflect instead of acting on emotion.

### *Common Crypto Scams and Clear Warning Signs*

The crypto world is full of shortcuts and traps. Pump-and-dump schemes are one of the oldest tricks. Imagine an online chat group suddenly claims a little-known coin will skyrocket. People rush in, the price jumps, then the original promoters dump their holdings, causing the price to collapse. Newcomers buy at the top, then watch their investment evaporate.

Fake tokens and knockoff coins often come with slick names or websites that look almost real. A beginner sees "Ethereum Plus," thinks it's connected with Ethereum, and sends their funds. The project vanishes a few weeks later.

Phishing is everywhere. You might get an email or message that seems to come from your exchange or wallet provider, urging you to act fast and click a link. The link leads to a site that looks just like the real thing, when you log in, scammers snag your password and empty your account.

Ponzi and pyramid schemes pop up, promising sky-high returns if you recruit others or lock in your coins. Someone you know insists they're making easy money and offers you a spot, but payments only last until new investors run out. The scheme collapses, leaving most with nothing.

Fraudulent giveaways on social media are common. A fake "celebrity" account might ask you to send one coin to get two back. Once you send your crypto, it's gone.

### Spotting the Red Flags

- Promises of guaranteed, outsized returns
- Urgent messages pushing you to act right away
- Requests for your private key or recovery phrase
- Websites with spelling errors, clunky layouts, or missing information
- Investments with complicated structures that aren't clearly explained
- Messages from unknown contacts insisting on secrecy or pressure

Default to caution. If something feels off, pause and double-check. Trust builds slowly, but one careless click can undo months of effort.

## *Avoiding Rookie Mistakes That Cause Big Losses*

Anonymous projects that promise significant breakthroughs can easily capture your attention. Many rug pulls begin this way; the creators vanish, and the project's funds disappear with them. Always google the project, scan crypto forums, and look for real names and team information.

Sending crypto to the wrong address is a classic error. Transactions are irreversible. Always copy and paste wallet addresses, check the first and last few characters, and send a small test amount before transferring larger sums.

Impatience trips up many beginners. Trying to buy the dip or catch the peak, people end up buying high and selling low. Automated alerts or reminders can help dampen the urge to act quickly.

Stored funds on exchanges are an easy target for hacks. Move long-term assets into secure wallets instead of leaving them online.

Chasing every new token burns through funds. Instead, start with small amounts, set clear goals for each investment, and stick to them.

Every year brings headlines of people losing life savings after sending crypto to scammers or betting on anonymous projects that disappear. Prevention starts with routine checks, steady habits, and a cool head. Protection isn't about technical tricks; it's about common sense, preparation, and knowing that you're always one step ahead when you choose caution over speed.

Now that we've unpacked the wild ups and downs of cryptocurrency, the emotional traps investors face, and practical ways to protect your money, you're better prepared to step into this fast-moving world with confidence. By understanding what drives crypto prices, managing your risk wisely, and spotting scams before they catch you off guard, you set yourself up for smarter choices and steadier progress. Remember, successful investing isn't about chasing every trend or reacting to every headline; it's about sticking to a clear plan, staying calm when markets shake, and learning as you go. With these tools in hand, you're ready to take the next steps toward building your crypto portfolio safely and thoughtfully.

# CHAPTER 9
# MAKING PASSIVE INCOME WITH CRYPTO

Just a few years ago, the idea of earning money from cryptocurrencies without actively trading or constantly monitoring markets was something only tech experts discussed. Fast forward to today, and passive income streams in crypto are now available to everyday people who want to build wealth without diving into complex charts or taking major risks.

As exciting as this sounds, the world of passive crypto earnings is full of choices and challenges that can feel overwhelming. How do you know which options are safe? Which opportunities are real, and which might be too good to be true?

This chapter explores the practical side of making your crypto work for you quietly in the background. It will show you how to approach these methods with a clear understanding of both the potential rewards and the hidden risks. The goal is to find steady, reliable ways to grow your digital assets while keeping control and caution at the forefront.

## Understanding Passive Crypto Income Methods and Platforms

Stepping into the world of passive income with crypto can feel like entering a maze of new faces, buzzwords, and tempting promises. The good news is you don't need to be an expert or a day trader to earn reliable, ongoing returns. Three of the most popular, and approachable, passive income methods are staking, yield farming, and liquidity pools. With the right guidance, these can offer steady rewards in exchange for helping to maintain the systems that power crypto.

### *Staking: Earning Rewards the Safe Way*

Staking is one of the simplest ways to earn passive crypto income. Certain blockchains need people to lock up their tokens to help run the network safely and process transactions. Anyone who owns these tokens can "stake" them, basically, let the network use them for a while. In return, you earn rewards as a thank you from the network itself.

Here's how staking might work for a beginner:

Imagine you have some ADA (the coin for the Cardano blockchain). You want to earn more ADA without selling or trading. You look for a staking option on your exchange, decide how much ADA to lock up, and follow three easy steps:

1. Select "Stake" in your crypto wallet or exchange.
2. Choose the amount to stake and confirm.
3. Wait while your ADA is staked for a certain period.

Every few days or weeks, you'll see a bit of extra ADA appear in your account as a reward. If you decide to unstake, you might have to wait a few days before you can spend or move your coins again. Rewards can vary, but the process is designed so you don't need to supervise it. Many newcomers choose staking because it's straightforward and doesn't require special knowledge or equipment.

### *Yield Farming: Chasing Higher, Variable Returns*

Yield farming can sound a little wild, but the core idea is simple. You lend your crypto or place it somewhere others can borrow or swap, then collect a share of the profits the platform makes. The keyword here is "yield", your earnings can change, and there's a bit more going on behind the curtain.

Suppose you decide to try yield farming on a platform using USDT (a stablecoin pegged to the US dollar). The process might look like this:

1. Move your USDT to a DeFi protocol's wallet.
2. Choose a lending pool or a yield farm.
3. Deposit your USDT.

Other users borrow your USDT, paying fees or interest to the protocol. The platform shares those profits with you, so your earnings can go up and down depending on activity. Yield farming often offers higher possible returns than staking, but you need to pay closer attention—yields can drop, the protocol could run into trouble, or interest rates can change unexpectedly.

### *Liquidity Pools: Powering Decentralized Trading*

Liquidity pools are shared baskets of crypto that make it possible for people to swap tokens without needing buyers or sellers lined up all the time. Anyone can add assets to these pools, usually on a DeFi platform. By doing so, you help others trade with ease and get paid a slice of trading fees when swaps happen.

Here's a relatable example:

You hold both ETH and USDC and put the same value of each into an ETH/USDC liquidity pool. The pool uses your crypto (and others' too), so when someone trades ETH for USDC, there's always enough of each. For helping, you get a share of the fees from each trade. Your role is like being a mini-bank that always offers cash on hand. Liquidity pools can handle big sums, but for beginners, many platforms offer guides and calculators so you can estimate your rewards.

### *Centralized vs. Decentralized Platforms*

Where you use these strategies has a big effect on your comfort and security. Centralized exchanges (CEX), like Coinbase or Binance, work a lot like regular banks. They hold your crypto for you, offer easy-to-use menus, and often have solid customer support. You just click "stake," and it happens in the background. The downside is you give up a bit of control, and if the platform has issues, you might not have a quick way out.

DeFi platforms, by contrast, put all the power and responsibility in your hands. You hold your wallet, make every decision, and see all the transactions "on chain." You can get more rewards, and there's no bank, but if you lose your keys or make a mistake, you're on your own. Since DeFi is open to everyone, you must be vigilant against scams and bad actors.

### Weighing the Choices

Choosing the right passive income method depends on your goals and your appetite for risk. it's familiar, and there's usually quick support. If you're more adventurous and want to dig deeper, DeFi options like yield farming or liquidity pools can pay more, but you'll need to do your homework on platform safety, understand the possible swings in earnings, and keep track of your crypto security.

These income streams look promising, but it's smart to explore deeper before locking up your assets. The next step is to look at what shapes safety and returns, making sure your path is both rewarding and secure.

## Evaluating APY, Risks, and Safety Before Investing

When you hear about people making passive income with crypto, the numbers can sound eye-popping. A website might promise an APY of 100%, 500%, or even 1000% if you deposit your coins into their pool or farm. APY, or annual percentage yield, is just a fancy way of saying how much your money might earn if you keep it locked up for a full year. If you deposit $1,000 somewhere that offers a 100% APY, the claim is that you'd have $2,000 after 12 months. This sounds exciting, but there's a catch: high APY often means high risk, sometimes even danger to your original funds.

To understand this, picture two banks. One is old, reliable, and offers modest interest. The other is brand new with neon signs, offering to double your money in a year. In the real world, that second bank would make you suspicious. Crypto works in much the same way. High APYs attract attention, just like get-rich-quick schemes you might have seen before, but rarely are these offers as smooth as they appear.

Platforms achieve these big numbers with risky projects or by giving you tokens that might not be worth much in the future. Imagine depositing money to earn rewards in a token you've never heard of, only to watch its value drop to almost nothing overnight. These types of losses may occur when a project's token lacks strong demand or when team members abuse their authority to create additional tokens arbitrarily.

There are more dangers. Some high APY pools can be outright scams. You might have heard terms like "rug pull," where the team running a project drains all the money and disappears. Other times, the platform might seem legitimate, but it turns out the team is anonymous. If no one knows who is behind the project, you have no way to hold them accountable. Real projects usually have a public team with clear social media profiles and a record of communicating with users.

Market swings can wipe out your gains. Say you join a pool with a 40% APY, but the price of the token you're rewarded with drops 90% during the year. Even after getting all your rewards, you might end up with less than you started. There's also a thing called liquidity risk. If everyone rushes to take out their money at once, the platform might freeze withdrawals, leaving you unable to move your coins. You'd be stuck and possibly watching your balance go down in value.

If a platform offers incredible rewards, always check how long it's been around. Crypto moves fast, but projects that have lasted at least a year and survived ups and downs often show they're more solid. Look for security audits. These are like financial health checkups for the code that runs the platform. You'll usually see these mentioned on the project's website or blog if they exist. Good platforms work with outside companies to review their smart contracts, then publish those results.

Before trusting a platform, try searching its name with the word "scam" or "review." See what other users say in forums or on social media. A solid reputation almost always leaves a trail of real reviews, honest complaints, and helpful advice. If you are unable to find much information about a platform, or if red flags consistently appear, consider it a warning sign.

Always start with a small amount. Treat your first deposit as an experiment. Watch what happens. Does the platform do what it promised? Is it easy to withdraw? If even a tiny test leaves you waiting for your money or confused by hidden rules, imagine how much more stressful it would be with serious funds at stake.

Understanding a few extra ideas helps you play safer. Liquidity pools and yield farms come with something called impermanent loss, where the value of your deposits can change in ways you don't expect if prices move a lot. Withdrawal delays or time-locks can keep you from getting your cash out when you need it. Smart contract risk means that bugs in the platform's computer code could drain the pool or freeze your funds permanently.

Here, a classic rule applies: if a crypto project promises returns that appear excessively high, they almost always are. Take time to read guides, learn basic terms, and ask questions. Slow, steady earning in crypto often beats jumping for the shiniest deal, helping you avoid costly mistakes and keep your learning journey on solid footing.

Now that you understand the main ways to earn passive income with crypto and the vital safety checks to keep your money secure, you're better equipped to start your journey wisely. Whether you choose the simplicity of staking or the higher potential rewards of yield farming and liquidity pools, remember that patience, research, and caution are your best tools. By taking small steps, verifying platforms, and staying aware of risks like scams or market swings, you can build a solid foundation for earning in this exciting space. With this knowledge, you're ready to explore opportunities confidently, setting yourself up not just to chase quick gains, but to grow your crypto steadily and securely over time.

CHAPTER 10

# TAXES, REGULATIONS, AND WHAT TO WATCH FOR

Have you ever wondered what really happens behind the scenes when you buy or sell cryptocurrency? Or why some transactions seem simple while others come with surprises such as extra paperwork or unexpected fees? How do governments track digital money that is not printed or controlled by banks?

These questions can leave even the most curious investors feeling uncertain about how to move forward with confidence. This chapter will guide you through the key rules and responsibilities connected to crypto investing. You will learn how to navigate this complex landscape, protect your profits, stay compliant with the law, and avoid common mistakes along the way.

## Crypto Taxation Essentials and Smart Tracking

For most beginners, the word "tax" can make cryptocurrency feel intimidating. Crypto might look and work like digital cash, but most countries treat it differently when it comes to taxes. Governments see cryptocurrencies as “property” or digital assets, not as money. This means selling, swapping, or even spending your coins can create something called a taxable event. Simply holding your crypto is not taxed; only certain actions trigger taxes.

Think of crypto like a valuable comic book or a rare sneaker. If you buy a sneaker and keep it on your shelf, there’s no tax. If you sell it later for more than you paid, you might owe tax on the profit. With crypto, taxable events usually include:

- Selling coins for cash (like turning Bitcoin into dollars)
- Trading one crypto for another (such as swapping Ethereum for Solana)
- Using crypto to buy something (for example, paying for coffee with Dogecoin)
- Getting paid in crypto for work or earning coins from mining

Whenever one of these events happens, you may owe taxes based on how much your coins changed in value. This is where “capital gains” come into play. "Capital gains" just means the profit you make when you sell or trade something for more than you paid for it. If you bought Bitcoin at $10,000 and sold it at $20,000, the $10,000 profit counts as a capital gain, which may be taxed.

Here’s another term you’ll see: “cost basis.” "Cost basis" means the original amount you spent on your crypto, including any fees. If you bought 1 Bitcoin for $10,000, that’s your cost basis. When you sell that Bitcoin, the difference between your cost basis and the selling price is your gain or loss. It works almost like keeping score in a game; what you started with versus what you ended up with tells you if you won or lost.

Taxable events do not happen when you buy crypto with regular money and just let it sit in your wallet. Nothing happens tax-wise until you sell, swap, or spend your coins. If you are rewarded with crypto, such as getting paid for a job, earning some from a staking program, or mining new coins, these are usually counted as regular income, just like if your job paid you in dollars.

## Basic Record-Keeping for Crypto Taxes

To keep things stress-free, build the habit of documenting every transaction. Accurate records make everything easier, both for reporting taxes and for keeping track of your profits and losses. You only need a few details for each trade or transfer:

- The date of the transaction
- The type and amount of cryptocurrency (e.g., 0.2 Bitcoin)
- The value in local currency at the time
- What happened (e.g., sold Bitcoin for cash, traded Ethereum for Litecoin)
- Any fees paid

You can start with a simple spreadsheet. Here is a basic layout: "Capital gains" helps eliminate the "Where did I buy that?" panic at tax time. Taking a minute to add a new row after every crypto move will save you many headaches later. If remembering is hard, set a phone reminder to update your log once a week.

## Helpful Tools for Tracking Transactions

Manual tracking works, but specialized tools can make life simpler. Popular tax-tracking apps and platforms such as Koinly, CoinTracker, and CryptoTaxCalculator are used by many beginners and seasoned investors alike.

These apps connect to your wallets and exchanges and automatically pull in your purchases, sales, swaps, and income. Most provide real-time dashboards that show what your portfolio is worth and label each transaction. When tax season rolls around, many can generate downloadable summaries or starter tax forms, which you or your accountant can use directly.

It feels overwhelming at first, but these tools break everything down into clear categories and numbers. You'll see all your crypto activity in one place. This not only lowers stress but also helps you catch errors, like a missed trade or a deposit you forgot to log. Despite the small fees associated with these services, many beginners find the peace of mind they provide to be worth it.

## Staying Calm and Building Good Habits

Most people worry about taxes when it's already time to file, which can create anxiety. The best way to avoid feeling swamped is to work in small batches all year long. You don't need to be perfect; just write down every trade and check your logs monthly. Use break reminders to prompt yourself. If you fall behind, update your records as soon as possible and do not let confusion grow.

Governments use tax laws to bring some order and predictability to the new world of digital assets. Tax rules don't just collect revenue; they protect honest investors as well. How do regulators make sure crypto stays fair and safe? Why are rules needed in a world built on freedom and innovation? These are questions every investor will start to see as their journey continues.

## Navigating Government Regulation and Staying Compliant

Imagine moving coins from one country to another, only to discover that local rules have changed overnight. Around the world, governments are developing new ways to monitor, control, or even encourage cryptocurrency adoption. For investors, understanding these rules isn't just about filing tax forms; every action, from trading to holding tokens, can depend on how local authorities see crypto. Take the United States: the government treats crypto as property, and new laws sometimes target exchanges with tougher identity checks or require all transactions above a certain value to be disclosed. Meanwhile, in El Salvador, Bitcoin is the official currency, meaning people can use it for payments anywhere. On the other side, China regularly steps in to limit trading, ban mining, or order exchange closures, making direct participation for ordinary people much harder.

Europe stands between these approaches. The European Union wants each member country to set basic crypto rules while working toward region-wide standards. In places like

Germany and Switzerland, investors find stronger protections and clear legal paths, provided they use regulated exchanges and stick to the rules. Many Asian countries, like Japan and South Korea, follow similar models, tightly licensing platforms but still supporting active trading. These contrasts matter for investors because local laws determine what wallets you can use, which exchanges allow you to open an account, and whether profits are legal to bring home. Even if you live in a country with loose oversight, using a popular global exchange could bring you under much stricter rules set by the exchange's home country.

Consider what happens when rules shift quickly. A government may suddenly demand that all users verify their identities before withdrawing funds. Some investors, unable or unwilling to provide documents, may lose access to their holdings for weeks or longer. In another situation, a regulator could demand that exchanges in their region delist certain tokens or stop doing business with other countries. This can disrupt trading, freeze assets, or force coins into complicated withdrawal processes that carry added risk or cost.

Common regulatory events often shake up investors with little warning. A country might ban anonymous wallets overnight, sending panic through the markets as people scramble to secure or transfer their coins. Unlicensed exchanges can shut down unexpectedly if found breaking rules, leaving customers scrambling to retrieve their funds. These situations reveal why most governments develop regulations: to limit scams, stop money laundering, trace criminal actions, or protect newcomers from getting burned by fraudulent offers.

Keeping compliant and safe means developing a few simple habits. Before sending funds or buying coins, always check an exchange's registration status. Legitimate platforms mention their approvals in public areas, like the front page or in their user agreements. Set a routine to scan for announcements in your exchange's news section or social media accounts. These updates often warn of policy changes, new verification needs, or deadlines for users to update their profiles.

## Legal Best Practices for Everyday Investors

1. Read and save the user agreement or compliance section from any platform you use.
2. Complete all requested "Know Your Customer" steps when prompted; uploading identity documents is now a standard process for most reputable exchanges.
3. Use only wallets and platforms that are registered or clearly regulated in your country or region.
4. Subscribe to official regulatory alerts or industry newsletters to spot new laws or scams.
5. Regularly review your exchange accounts for compliance notices, and make sure your account details are current.
6. Make a habit of moving funds only when you're confident the transaction won't break local laws. When in doubt, seek guidance from a trusted professional or legal advisor.

Stay sharp when presented with "too good to be true" investment offers. These often come from platforms with no physical address, no named management, or vague company details. Red flags also include exchanges that never ask for identification or force you to move funds via untraceable methods. When uncertain, stick with well-known brands that remain transparent about their headquarters, registration, and company owners.

Linking regulatory awareness to profit protection is straightforward. If an investor misses a new rule or deadline, funds may stay locked in limbo during a regulatory crackdown. Acting quickly when governments raise the bar, such as by finishing new verification steps or auditing which tokens are legal to trade, can mean the difference between having usable assets and joining a line of customers waiting for their coins. Smart investors treat regulation as part of everyday portfolio management, not just as a yearly tax exercise or rare emergency step. This approach builds a habit of checking compliance as naturally as tracking prices, making profits last, and avoiding risks that turn potential gains into costly lessons.

Now that you understand how taxes and regulations shape the world of crypto investing, you're better equipped to navigate this exciting but complex space with confidence. By keeping clear records, using helpful tracking tools, and staying alert to changing rules, you can protect your profits and avoid costly mistakes. Remember, smart investing isn't just about choosing the right coins. It's also about following the laws and building habits that keep you compliant and secure. With these foundations in place, you're ready to move forward on your crypto journey, making informed decisions that help your investments grow safely and sustainably.

# CHAPTER 11
# WHERE CRYPTO IS HEADED NEXT

Have you ever wondered what the future holds for cryptocurrency and digital assets? With so many new terms, technologies, and trends emerging, it's easy to feel overwhelmed or unsure about where to focus your attention. How can you tell which developments are meaningful and which are just passing hype? What should you look for to invest wisely and avoid common pitfalls? These questions are becoming more important as crypto moves beyond niche communities into mainstream finance and everyday life.

This chapter will explore the key movements shaping crypto's future and offer practical ways to stay informed and make smart decisions. You'll learn about the forces driving change in digital ownership, virtual worlds, and institutional involvement. We'll also cover how to find reliable information, evaluate new projects carefully, and build habits that help you navigate this fast-changing landscape with confidence. Whether you're entirely new or just cautious about jumping in, this guide aims to give you clear steps toward understanding and participating in the next phase of cryptocurrency.

## Emerging Trends and Future Technologies in Crypto

Everyday life is becoming more connected to digital assets, shifting the way value, identity, and opportunity flow through technology. At the core of this shift are three forces. Web3 brings new ways to own and control online identity, the metaverse turns digital activity into true experience and property, and institutional investment signals that crypto is not just hype but a maturing part of the economy. Even people brand new to cryptocurrency will feel the changes brought by these trends.

Web3 stands for a new version of the internet built on blockchains. Unlike earlier platforms where big companies hold your data and accounts, Web3 spreads control out across networks, giving power back to individual users. Imagine logging into a website or app, not with a standard username, but by connecting a digital wallet that stores your unique identity and assets. No company can take it away, freeze it, or use your details for hidden profit. If you buy a song or game item as an NFT, you actually own it. You can sell, lend, or gift it without risking deletion when a company shuts down. For young professionals, this can mean controlling your professional reputation or creative work, for investors it opens the door to new types of ownership, no longer bound by the rules of banks or large tech platforms.

Layered into this vision is the rise of the metaverse, a network of virtual worlds where people work, play, and do business with real stakes. Instead of just browsing the web or checking an app, users can meet in 3D spaces, own land, or operate businesses using digital currency. Leading companies and small developers alike are pouring energy into these new experiences. Crypto and NFTs tie directly to these digital worlds. Picture buying a wearable outfit for your avatar, securing a virtual desk job in an office that pays in cryptocurrency, or attending a live concert where tickets are blockchain-verified to prevent scams. These are not sci-fi fantasies. Already, fashion labels sell virtual clothes, real estate changes hands inside games, and social lives blend with crypto-powered communities. For anyone weary of traditional work or searching for new markets, the metaverse blurs the line between play and profit.

Not everything in crypto relies on buzz or fringe communities. Some of the world's largest banks, funds, and payment outlets now create real-world gateways into digital assets. When long-standing names start buying and holding cryptocurrencies, launching trading services, or building related products, it marks a shift from decentralized hobbyists to mainstream finance. Take a look at recent headlines: Payment companies add the option to buy crypto alongside dollars. Hedge funds and retirement groups allocate a slice of holdings to Bitcoin or Ethereum, treating them with the same seriousness as stocks. This growing interest doesn't just bring new money. It steers the industry toward greater security rules and risk checks while also building trust among cautious first-time buyers. The change is driving more stable prices, better safeguards, and reliable practices, all signals that the wild-west days of crypto are giving way to a more grounded, widely accepted system.

Ethereum, as one of the key platforms at the heart of these changes, offers a striking example of technical evolution. Most early cryptocurrencies, including Bitcoin, use what's called proof-of-work. This means powerful computers have to solve difficult puzzles to add records to the blockchain, burning lots of energy and favoring those with expensive machines. Ethereum has started switching to proof-of-stake. Under this system, anyone with coins can help run the network just by "staking" them, a bit like leaving cash in a secure box to support the system, and receive rewards in return. There is no need for special gear or sky-high electricity bills. More people can join in, reducing barriers and saving energy. For instance, a college student with $500 worth of Ethereum can stake it and earn small returns, while a large investor can do the same with much larger sums.

On top of this, Ethereum keeps rolling out updates that target speed, cost, and how many transactions can run at once. Recent improvements aim to lower fees when using decentralized apps, expand the types of deals that smart contracts can handle, and lessen technical roadblocks for both users and creators. These upgrades make it easier to launch new DeFi apps for borrowing, lending, or insuring assets, as well as supporting creative uses like digital art and music NFTs.

All these forces, including decentralized control with Web3, creative experiences in the metaverse, trusted financial backing from major institutions, and the technological advances of Ethereum, work together to drive progress. They increase adoption, create new ways for people to participate, and help reduce some of the older risks.

At the same time, important questions remain. Can these developments make crypto safer for everyone, or will new risks emerge? How will regulations keep up, and what happens when large financial players interact with small online communities?

Whether you are new to crypto or have been involved for years, staying informed and adaptable is essential. The pace of change guarantees both surprises and opportunities in the road ahead.

## Staying Informed and Navigating Crypto's Rapid Change Responsibly

Stepping from the latest headlines about Ethereum and Web3, readers soon realize that knowing where crypto is headed takes more than staying on top of a news cycle. Each new feature, protocol, or digital asset launches with excitement, and old rules shift quickly. Adapting to this pace means setting up daily habits for learning and balancing enthusiasm with care.

A solid starting point is building a list of reliable information outlets. Instead of jumping from social media rumor to rumor, turn to sources valued for transparency, research, and community feedback.

### Trusted Crypto News & Analysis

- CoinDesk: latest news and opinion
- The Block: headlines and market analysis
- Decrypt: educational explainers, industry updates

### Research Platforms

- Messari: in-depth project reports and analytics
- Glassnode: blockchain data, investor trends

### Official Blogs

- Ethereum Foundation, Solana Foundation: direct from the protocol's teams

Different people learn in different ways, so beyond websites, explore other tools to make learning stick.

- **Newsletters:** Curated newsletters give quick daily or weekly updates. The Pomp Letter and Bankless help readers catch key trends without sifting through endless feeds.
- **Podcasts:** "Unchained" by Laura Shin and "Crypto Top Trading Signals" bring market analysis and interviews directly to your earbuds.
- **YouTube Channels:** DataDash or Coin Bureau explain trends in plain language for visual learners.

Not every valuable lesson comes from a news site or media personality. Community spaces fill knowledge gaps and let beginners ask questions with less fear of being out of place.

**Online Forums and Groups:**

- Reddit's r/CryptoCurrency and r/ethfinance
- Discord servers run by blockchain projects or focused on trading

**Offline Opportunities:**

- Local crypto meetups, seminars, or even live conferences

In community chats, real experiences and warning stories mix with fast tips about emerging scams or smart contract flaws, grounding recent headlines with firsthand insight.

As the market shifts, so do popular projects, and it is tempting to chase the next big thing. Instead, move slowly and use a structured approach to test value and reduce risk.

### *Four Steps for Evaluating New Projects*

1. **Read the Whitepaper:** Check for clear explanations and defined problems. Is it easy to follow or full of vague promises?
2. **Research the Team:** Search for their public work, past projects, and their visibility in the industry.
3. **Analyze Utility & Tokenomics:** Identify what the token does, its distribution, and any built-in incentives or red flags like unchecked minting.
4. **Cross-Reference Experts & Community:** Look for expert opinion pieces, and see how communities discuss the project openly.

When Ethereum competitors like Solana or Cardano appeared, early investors compared testnet activity, developer engagement, and actual product use, not just announcements. NFT collectibles like CryptoPunks drew sustained interest not because they were hyped, but because of traceable ownership, visible developers, and lasting communities. These are examples of "trust but verify."

With swift information comes noise, and even experienced readers feel lost or overwhelmed. A helpful routine is to schedule a regular "learning audit." Every week, set aside time to:

- Review the top news stories that may affect your holdings.
- Check the latest project updates or white papers of assets you hold.
- Evaluate your portfolio's performance and any biases (such as holding too much of one token).
- Delete or stop following sources that cause anxiety, distractions, or seem to chase clicks over facts.

Think of this like preparing for travel. You don't book a trip based on a single ad or post. Instead, you read reviews, check official sites, ask friends, and compare prices. In crypto, each source offers part of the story. Only a full picture can guide you safely.

Exploring new tokens and platforms asks for a mix of curiosity and skepticism. Remember the many DeFi "rug pulls," where charismatic teams vanished with funds. Look out for "too good to be true" returns or coins promoted by celebrities with no track record. When emotions run high and crowds race to buy in, your strongest safeguard is to pause, verify details, and stick to a checklist.

Every reader brings different goals, timelines, and comfort levels. Write down your risk tolerance and what you hope to achieve, whether it's steady growth, supporting a cause, or funding a future purchase. Keep a "learning and investing checklist" close by with points like

- Did I research this project beyond social media?
- Am I risking more than I can lose?
- Is my decision based on evidence or fear of missing out?

This checklist will help anchor actions to a thoughtful plan and keep excitement productive, rather than reckless.

Staying ahead in crypto is not a sprint for hot tips. It's a habit of constant learning, careful filtering, structured evaluation, and honest self-reflection. This process gives any reader the confidence to participate wisely, no matter what the next headline promises.

Now that we understand the key trends and strategies shaping cryptocurrency's future, from Web3 and the metaverse to institutional involvement and evolving platforms like Ethereum, we are better equipped to navigate this fast-changing world with confidence. Embracing a habit of ongoing learning, careful research, and thoughtful evaluation will help you separate real opportunities from hype and risks. By staying informed through trusted sources, engaging with communities, and following a structured approach to investing, you can take control of your digital journey and make smarter choices. The path ahead may be full of surprises, but with clear guidance and steady curiosity, you're ready to participate wisely and turn today's innovations into tomorrow's possibilities.

# CHAPTER 12
# YOUR CRYPTO GAME PLAN

"Where do I even start with crypto?" It's a question many newcomers ask as they scan endless posts, tweets, and videos promising quick riches. The cryptocurrency world can seem like a confusing maze, filled with loud voices pulling you in different directions. Without a clear plan, it's easy to feel overwhelmed or make decisions based on hype and fear.

Developing a practical game plan is the key to navigating this fast-moving market with confidence. This chapter guides you through setting clear goals that match your comfort with risk and time commitment, building steady learning habits, and finding reliable sources of information. You'll also discover how to connect with supportive communities and take thoughtful action, so you can move forward without getting lost in noise or falling for scams. With a solid strategy in place, the path to smart crypto investing becomes clearer and more manageable.

## Goal-Setting and Lifelong Learning Strategies

Stepping into the world of cryptocurrency can feel like standing at the edge of a maze. For beginners, it's easy to get swept up in bold promises and rapid-fire opinions that flood the internet. That's why building your own crypto game plan comes first. Before buying any coin or following the crowd. Your plan centers your decisions, helps you stay disciplined during wild price swings, and guards you from making snap judgments based on fear or excitement. Here, the focus lands on setting real goals, building learning habits, and knowing where to find honest information. This way, you keep your journey organized and grounded from day one.

People enter crypto for all sorts of reasons. Some individuals aspire to engage in trading as a means of generating rapid profits, closely monitoring the minute-by-minute movements of prices and anticipating profits during the subsequent surge. Others take a calmer approach, investing small amounts over months or years to watch them grow. Many start just to learn how digital currencies work, curious about blockchain and eager to experiment. It's common to feel pulled in several directions at once, so the first step is asking yourself, "Why am I here?"

Sit down and write what you hope to achieve. Are you hoping to save for a trip, dreaming of retirement income, or simply curious about the buzz? Think about your comfort with risk. How would you feel if your $100 shrank to $60 overnight? How much time are you willing to dedicate? Five minutes a day, or an hour each week? Be honest, and put it on paper. For example, you might write, "I plan to buy and hold $200 in

Bitcoin and Ethereum for at least 12 months," or "My goal is to learn how exchanges work, so I'll make one small transaction per month." These statements keep you focused when social media is hyping the latest coin. They advise you to maintain your own pace and resist the temptation to act quickly when prices rise or fall.

Clear goals are more than just good intentions. They influence all your future decisions, from what platforms you join to what research you do. A well-defined plan cuts down on emotional trading and helps you resist the pressure to follow trends or online "gurus." It gives you permission to learn at your speed and to say "no" to risky bets that don't fit your aims.

Once you have your reason for entering crypto, the next piece is learning. On a schedule that works for you. The crypto landscape constantly changes. New coins launch, regulations shift, and scams pop up overnight. The best way to stay ahead is to form steady habits. Try dedicating 15 minutes a day to checking a trusted crypto news site, or schedule an hour on Sundays to read about a concept you don't yet grasp, such as how a wallet works or what blockchain actually means. Even short, regular sessions will help you filter out noise and spot patterns.

False claims and fake "experts" spring up everywhere. Learn how to spot red flags. If someone guarantees profits, claims to have secret knowledge, or pushes you to act urgently ("Buy now or miss out!"), pause and investigate. No one can promise gains in this market. Be careful with influencers who show off their wealth or refuse to explain their reasoning. Their goal is often attention, not your education. Social media trends can lure beginners into risky projects based on excitement, not facts.

Curiosity is your best defense against hype. Don't just trust a single source. Double-check what you read. If you see a claim that a new token will triple in value, search for details from at least two other places, such as established news sites or well-known analysts. Reliable news outlets often present both sides of a story, showing potential gains and possible drawbacks. When someone simply shouts about the "next big thing," compare it to a resource that patiently explains how the project works, its track record, and risks.

Here is how the difference might look:

- A flashy influencer on a video says, "Double your money in days with this secret coin!"
- A trusted analyst writes, "This project has potential but also serious risks, such as low trading volume and unclear leadership."

If you make decisions based on the first message, you risk losing funds on an unproven scheme. By choosing the second, you learn to weigh both positives and negatives. Use multiple sources before acting, and avoid echo chambers where only one view is allowed.

This focus on clear goal-setting, steady habits, and careful source-checking forms the strong base for moving forward. With your plan in hand and your mind attuned to quality information, the path ahead becomes more manageable. Soon, you can turn your goals into action by finding supportive communities and trustworthy resources to help you keep learning without losing your way in the noise.

## Connecting, Staying Updated, and Taking Action

Cryptocurrency can feel like a noisy, confusing crowd full of big promises and urgent warnings. To make wise choices, it helps to not only rely on your skills but also tap into supportive communities and trusted resources. When someone first enters the crypto world, it's easy to lose themselves in the excitement or succumb to skepticism. A smart game plan involves surrounding yourself with reliable voices and clear information while learning how to judge the difference between solid advice and empty hype.

### *Finding the Right Crypto Community*

Communities offer more than just tips or the latest price predictions. They can be a shield against scams and a support system for real learning. A healthy crypto community shares ideas in a respectful way. Members listen, answer beginner questions patiently, and value honesty. When someone posts a question about wallets or security, helpful replies focus on clear explanations, not just "buy now" promotions or referral links. Good communities also make their rules clear from the start, and there's always some kind of moderation to keep conversations safe. Scammers and aggressive promoters are dealt with quickly, and everyone knows that quick-rich schemes are not welcome. In a trusted space, you won't find bullying or people mocking those who make mistakes. Instead, experienced users step in to help without pushing anyone toward risky trading or coins nobody understands. Local meetups and online groups can both offer real connections, but always check how the group responds to new members before joining in fully.

### *Picking Trusted Crypto Resources*

Quality resources help you build confidence step by step. Clear online tutorials, beginner-friendly books with positive reviews, and widely recognized education platforms stand out. When a book or website uses simple language, shows both benefits and risks, and covers topics from wallets to security, it becomes valuable over time. Be wary of flashy sites that push courses promising "guaranteed profits" or recommend coins about to "explode." Instead, look for lessons that help you think for yourself, such as analyzing blockchain explorers, reading actual whitepapers, or breaking down how a project's technology works. Official blogs and developer forums can be excellent for deep dives, but always check who is posting and whether the content is updated regularly. Resources that gloss over the difficult aspects or concentrate primarily on persuading you to purchase their own product should cause concern. The best resources show you how to check facts for yourself, so you're less dependent on the next guru or social media "influencer."

### *Spotting Reliable Crypto News*

Staying up to date is important, but it matters where your news comes from. A trusted crypto news outlet names its authors, shows their background, and includes links to sources and official statements. Articles focus on the facts, such as changes in regulation, adoption by companies, or security incidents, without wild predictions. You'll see transparency about advertisers and clear lines between news and opinion. If you come across a government decision that impacts cryptocurrency, it's important to consult reputable sites that provide a clear explanation, include quotes from both sides, and refrain from declaring that a crash is imminent or that prices are skyrocketing. In contrast, sites that use clickbait headlines, urge you to trade fast, or mention secret insider tips are often looking for quick clicks or have hidden sponsors. When news breaks, compare a few reliable sources rather than rushing to act on the first alert.

### *Avoiding Information Overload*

Crypto moves fast, but you don't have to chase every update. Having too many apps or news feeds makes decision-making harder. To keep your focus, limit yourself to a handful of trusted communities and sources. Turn off alerts that aren't urgent, and set times each week when you'll check in for updates and research. Keep a personal list of your "go-to" sites and communities, so you're not tempted by strangers or random tips. Fewer, better sources mean less stress and clearer thinking.

### *Actionable Crypto Checklist*

1. Pick one beginner-friendly crypto community and make an introduction post.
2. Bookmark two reputable crypto news sites and sign up for their weekly digests.
3. Choose an online tutorial or book that explains key crypto concepts and review one lesson per week.
4. Make a list of common red flags for scams: pushy private messages, guarantees of quick profits, unclear project details, or secret insider info.
5. Create a folder for official project links, white papers, or educational resources that you trust most.
6. Turn off non-essential notifications and schedule two sessions per week to catch up on news.
7. Practice checking the source of every major headline before reacting or sharing.
8. Share something helpful or ask a thoughtful question in your chosen community to start building positive connections.

A strong community, quality resources, and reliable news set the foundation for a calm, confident crypto journey. With a simple plan and steady habits, taking control of your learning becomes possible, letting you move forward with clarity instead of confusion.

Now that you've learned how to set clear goals, build steady learning habits, and find trustworthy communities and resources, you're ready to take confident steps in the cryptocurrency world. With a practical plan and reliable information guiding your decisions, you can avoid common pitfalls and stay focused on what matters most. By connecting with supportive groups and checking facts carefully, you'll navigate this fast-changing space with calm and clarity. Remember, success in crypto doesn't come from chasing every trend but from thoughtful action and continuous learning, so keep your goals in sight and move forward steadily toward your own version of success.

# BE THE VOICE THAT GUIDES THE NEXT INVESTOR FORWARD

At the heart of life, we rise by lifting others. Every time we share our experiences, we create a **bridge for someone who is just starting out**.

Think back. How did you feel when you first heard about *cryptocurrency*? **Excited? Confused? Unsure where to begin?**

Now imagine a beginner standing at that same crossroads, overwhelmed by talk of *Bitcoin, Ethereum, NFTs,* and all the rest. They're eager to learn but don't know which resources to trust.

That's where **your review** comes in. By leaving your *honest thoughts*, you help future readers see whether this guide gave you the **clarity, confidence, and strategies** they're looking for.

Your words can have a **ripple effect**. Making sure another curious beginner doesn't give up too soon but instead takes their **first smart step into crypto investing**.

**Thank you** so much for reading, learning, and now *considering sharing your voice*. Together, we can make the world of cryptocurrency more approachable, **one review at a time**.

# CONCLUSION

You've reached the final page of this book, but your journey into the world of cryptocurrency is just beginning. If you made it here, chances are you're still a little curious, maybe even excited, and perhaps, like most people at this stage, a bit cautious. That's wonderful. In crypto, curiosity drives discovery, and caution keeps your savings safe. No matter what you've read elsewhere, you don't have to be a tech wizard or financial genius to take part in this new frontier. You just need an open mind, a willingness to learn, and a plan.

Let's look back at what you've accomplished so far. You now know what Bitcoin and Ethereum are and why these digital assets matter beyond their price tags. You understand the basics of blockchain technology, not through dense jargon but in clear, practical terms. You've learned how to create your first wallet, store your private keys securely, and navigate exchanges confidently without getting lost in hype or confusing acronyms. Most importantly, you now have the tools to make your first investment wisely, balancing opportunity with risk and caution with optimism.

In a world overflowing with information, some helpful and much of it misleading, you chose to focus on clarity and simplicity. That choice matters. Many people stay on the sidelines because they believe crypto is too complicated or think that missing the early days means it's too late to start. The truth is much more encouraging: there is always room for newcomers. Every day, ordinary people who take the time to learn, ask questions, and act with intention create new possibilities.

Crypto investing isn't about chasing the wildest headlines or trying to predict the next overnight sensation. It's about understanding the fundamentals, protecting your assets, and making strategic decisions that fit your life. That's why throughout this book, we focused less on picking "the best coin" and more on giving you the confidence to choose for yourself, backed by real knowledge instead of gut feelings or online rumors.

Now, you stand at the edge of a genuine financial revolution. Digital assets are challenging long-held ideas about money, ownership, and trust. Decentralized finance (DeFi), non-fungible tokens (NFTs), and smart contracts are no longer just buzzwords; they are reshaping industries as diverse as art, music, gaming, and banking. Even if you only begin with a small investment, you are part of something much larger than yourself. This space is still young, and everyone, including experts, is learning as they go. That makes it exciting, but it also leaves room for mistakes. Staying grounded in research and skepticism, rather than acting out of fear of missing out, is your greatest strength.

If you remember one lesson from these pages, let it be this: crypto is not an all-or-nothing gamble. You are free to start small, no matter what trends or influencers suggest. Your security comes from understanding the basics well, from double-checking wallet addresses before transfers, keeping seed phrases offline, and never sharing private keys, to using strong passwords and enabling two-factor authentication. These small habits, practiced consistently, will protect your assets far better than any promise of instant riches.

But safety doesn't mean staying on the sidelines forever. Most experienced investors began with a single step - their first Bitcoin, a fraction of Ethereum, or a carefully chosen altcoin. Risks exist, but so do opportunities. By reading this book, you've already set yourself apart from many who jump in blindly or give up too soon. You now have a clear foundation for thoughtful, confident action. here to stay

Remember, markets rise and fall, but the transformative potential of blockchain technology is. Some coins will disappear, others will thrive, and new innovations will continue to emerge. That's part of what makes this field both challenging and rewarding. The people who benefit most are those who combine curiosity with caution and boldness with preparation, qualities you've strengthened throughout this learning journey.

Keep reaching for reliable sources, join trustworthy communities, ask clear questions, and share what you learn. Every year, new scams and get-rich-quick schemes appear, but better tools for research and protection also emerge. Staying informed is a lifelong process, not a one-time task. Don't be afraid to adjust your strategies as the landscape evolves. That's what the best investors do. Success in crypto, as in anything else, comes from steady growth, not shortcuts.

Let's talk about what happens next. Maybe you feel ready to buy your first coin, or perhaps you want to practice setting up wallets and trying out small transactions. Wherever you are, start simple. Choose one reputable exchange, one secure wallet, and one clear goal for your first purchase, whether it's holding long-term, experimenting with DeFi, or learning how transfers work. Write down your reasons, track your experiences, and review them regularly. These early steps will teach you more than any article or influencer ever could.

If you hit a roadblock or worry that you've made a mistake, remember that everyone was a beginner once. The most successful crypto investors aren't the ones who picked the right coin first; they're the ones who kept learning, adapted when necessary, and stayed patient during uncertain times. Progress may feel slow, but every small step builds confidence and knowledge. The fact that you've taken the time to educate yourself already places you ahead of most people.

Looking forward, the future of crypto is unwritten. Challenges will come, but so will opportunities for creativity, freedom, and growth that traditional finance could never offer. Whether your goal is long-term wealth building, portfolio diversification, supporting innovation, or simply becoming more financially aware, you already have the tools to begin.

So here's your first real challenge: don't wait until you feel completely ready. Start with one carefully chosen coin, one secure wallet, and one clear goal. Take a deep breath, double-check your steps, and take action today. The new financial frontier rewards those who are prepared, not those who wait for perfection. The most important thing is to begin.

This is your invitation to join a movement that's transforming how the world views money and value. None of us knows exactly what the next decade will bring, but we do know it will reward the curious, the cautious, and the courageous. The path ahead is yours to explore. Welcome to the new financial frontier.

COMPLE

www.ingramcontent.com/pod-product-compliance
Lightning Source LLC
Chambersburg PA
CBHW050529240926
51846CB00003B/749
* 9 7 8 1 9 7 0 8 3 9 1 3 5 *